Credit

Credit and Debt

Sorting it out

Michael Schluter
and
David Lee

Marshall Pickering

Marshall Morgan and Scott
Marshall Pickering
34–42 Cleveland Street, London, W1P 5FB, UK

Copyright © 1989 Michael Schluter and David Lee
First published in 1989 by Marshall Morgan and Scott Publications Ltd
Part of the Marshall Pickering Holdings Group

British Library CIP Data

Schluter, Michael, and Lee, David
  Credit and debt: sorting it out
  1. England. Consumers. Debts. Payment – Manuals
  I. Title   II. Lee, David
  332.024′02

  ISBN: 0 551 01780 5

Text set in Baskerville by Avocet Robinson, Buckingham
Printed in Great Britain by Cox & Wyman Ltd, Reading, Berks.

Contents

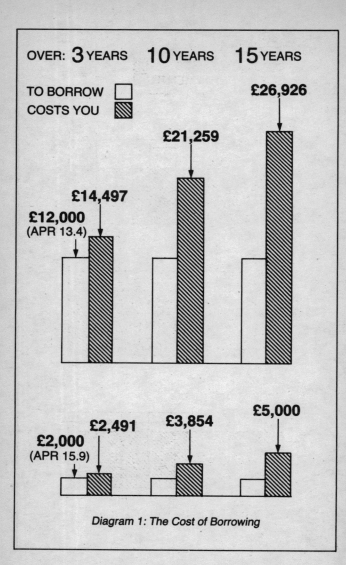

OVER: **3** YEARS   **10** YEARS   **15** YEARS

TO BORROW ☐
COSTS YOU ▨

£26,926

£21,259

£14,497

£12,000
(APR 13.4)

£5,000

£3,854

£2,491

£2,000
(APR 15.9)

Diagram 1: The Cost of Borrowing

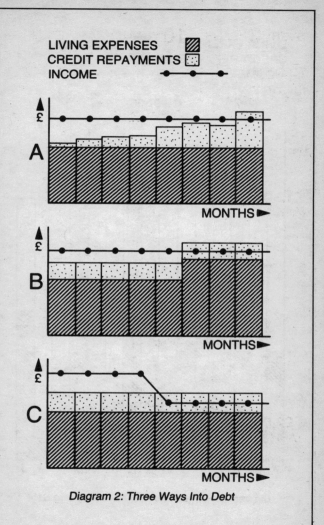

LIVING EXPENSES
CREDIT REPAYMENTS
INCOME

A

MONTHS ▶

B

MONTHS ▶

C

MONTHS ▶

Diagram 2: Three Ways Into Debt

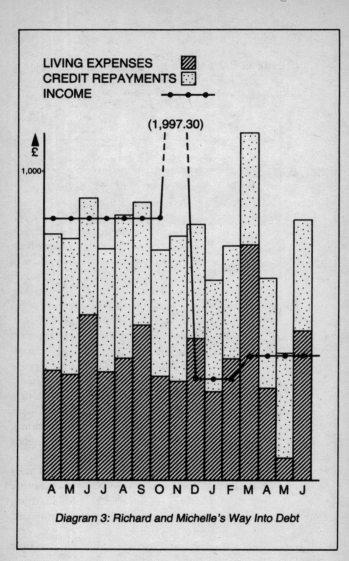

LIVING EXPENSES
CREDIT REPAYMENTS
INCOME

(1,997.30)

£

1,000-

A M J J A S O N D J F M A M J

Diagram 3: Richard and Michelle's Way Into Debt

Chapter 1

Living on the Knife Edge

Jim and Deborah Curtis

Jim and Deborah Curtis were successful.

Both had full-time jobs. Jim, who worked in a factory, often did fifteen hours' overtime on the weekend. On top of that he had one or two little sidelines going, earning a tenner here and there doing removals in his transit, and as much as a hundred a week selling personal computers. If you'd asked Jim and Deborah what they made in a month the answer would have been something close to a thousand pounds, as much as half again what they received as a basic wage.

Perhaps because they prided themselves on being better off than their neighbours they spent freely, and weren't afraid to take goods home on credit. Why wait when work was secure and they knew they could cover the repayments? Eventually they'd collected so many plastic cards that the whole business of spending turned into a bit of a joke. One card for jewellery, one for photography, one for furniture, one for decorating. And no one ever asked them if they could afford the goods they were buying – their credit clearance was sky high.

The Curtises gave scant thought to budgeting. If they thought about it at all it was only to remark to one another how little they had to pay every month to enjoy life's luxuries. They felt wealthy, and expected this feeling to last, undisturbed, for the rest of their lives.

But then Jim's firm hit the recession. First the overtime

went. Then the bottom fell out of his computer market. In a matter of a few months the Curtis' income dropped by three or four hundred pounds. For the first time, Jim decided to add up all the money he was paying out in credit commitments. He made an unpleasant discovery: he was further in debt than he'd thought.

Initially he met the shortfall by selling assets and replacing them on credit. This didn't work for long; soon he found himself juggling the cards, drawing on one account to pay into another, and all the time falling further behind on his payments. In the end he decided to go the the bank. The manager refused him the £4,000 loan he was asking for, but did give him £1,000, which Jim used to pull his accounts back into the black.

Unfortunately the respite was short-lived. There were several reasons for this. One was that Jim and Deborah continued to use their credit cards. The habit of buying was hard to break. But even when they tried to break it, by conrolling their spending, they faced further, unforseen expenses. Jim's motorbike was stolen. Their daughter got married. There were dental bills. And so Jim was forced to return to the bank. This time the manager was more understanding; he let them go overdrawn, extended their loan to £2,000, to £4,000, then to £6,000.

After a couple of years the sums they owed – to the bank, and on their various credit accounts – were growing so fast that Jim's attempts to pay off the creditors no longer kept pace with the interest. When Deborah's father died and left them £5,000, the money was simply swallowed up in repayments. This time Jim and Deborah could see no solution. Looking back they realised they'd been living on the knife edge for years, pledging a future income they couldn't guarantee for goods they could have done without. Now it was too late.

They had strayed into debt – and the door had closed behind them.

Chapter 2

Who Do They Think You Are?

Jim and Deborah's story is true. We've changed names, and details in order to protect the identity of the people involved. But the situation is real and it's still going on.

How do you react to it?

It may be that you have had an experience similar to theirs. If so, you may be thinking, 'Yes, I can sympathise with them – I know what it's like to be in debt.'

On the other hand, if their experience is strange to you, you may be thinking, 'Thank goodness I'm free of debt, and not in the same mess as they are.'

Possibly you're having both reactions at the same time, fear and gladness, anxiety and relief. But most people will want to put themselves in one group or the other. Either they'll frankly admit they're in trouble, or they'll insist they're doing fine, and regard themselves as spectators, looking on at debt from the sidelines.

Clearly this book is intended to help people in the first group. But if you're in the second group, take care. It's a fact that many spectators of debt will sooner or later find themselves down on the pitch. For debt is not, as is often thought. a situation – it is a process; not a place so much as a road down which you are travelling. And this means that many people who think they're financially secure are heading into debt just as surely as the 10.50 from Birmingham New Street is heading into Euston.

Jim and Deborah Curtis were in this kind of situation

for years before their debts finally caught up with them. They describe it themselves as 'living on the knife edge'. Another phrase for it might be 'living beyond your means'.

People on the knife edge make ample use of credit, and may always have been what financiers call *creditworthy*. But they are increasingly hard put to meet the repayments; they are tempted to borrow again to cover what seems to be a recurring shortfall of cash. In spite of resolutions to control their spending they may even have defaulted once or twice on the credit card account, and so made the short transition from credit to debt.

The point is this:

Serious debt isn't something that happens to other people. Debt can happen to *you*.

Credit and debt

It's worth emphasising here the difference between *credit* and *debt*.

Credit allows us to enjoy the benefit of goods or services before we have actually paid for them. It is very common; over half the homes purchased in Britain are purchased on credit – that is, with the help of a mortgage – and, once housed, nine out of ten people take their gas and electricity on credit, settling up after a quarterly meter reading has determined the payment due.

That being the case, you could say that credit turns into debt only if you fail to meet the financial commitment on time. But from the consumer's point of view it is more realistic to regard *any money owed to others* as being a debt. Not that borrowing is always unwise. A mortgage, for instance, although involving large amounts of money, is a loan based on what is usually an appreciating asset; in other words, if you cannot maintain your repayments you can almost certainly sell the house for more than you paid for it. But the same reasoning cannot be applied to most furniture and electrical equipment. These are *depreciating* assets, goods that lose their value over time, and in the end become virtually worthless. The fact that most people buy such goods on credit as willingly as they'd buy a house shows how little consideration the average consumer gives to his financial wellbeing. If credit cards were called DEBT CARDS he might think twice.

As it is, serious debt is widespread in Britain. To use again the examples of housing and power; an estimated 300,000 people are more than three months in arrears on their mortgage repayments; and every year over a million have difficulty paying their gas or electricity bills. That is alarming enough. What makes it even more so is the fact that debt in Britain is on the increase as it has never been before.

In real terms (in other words, when inflation has been accounted for), the total amount of money owed by British people to banks, finance companies and building societies has doubled between 1980 and 1986. And most of the increase has occurred in the eighties. Quite apart from the effect of this change on ordinary people like Jim and Deborah Curtis, it could be said that debt is fast becoming a national problem.

Of course people get into debt for a great variety of reasons; there is, as the saying goes, more than one route to the top of the mountain. But one major influence on the way we use credit – and thus on the ease with which we fall into debt – is advertising, and that is where we are going to begin in this book.

If it seems a strange place to start from, think for a moment how it was that you were first encouraged to take out, say, a bank loan or a credit account. Almost certainly,

15

advertising will have been instrumental. In fact, you have to hand it to the advertisers: they have produced a revolutionary change in the way British people think about credit. The day was when the man or woman in the street looked on hire purchase – an early form of credit agreement – with caution, even distaste; now they consider it not only permissible but prestigious to 'pay by card'.

How did the advertisers do it? And how can understanding the process help us sort out debt?

Credit advertising and what it offers you

Take a walk down your local high street, buy a copy of a local or tabloid newspaper, and pick up a selection of pamphlets on credit and loans from shops and banks.

You will now be armed with the latest equipment, straight from the advertisers' front line. Between them these publications represent the four major sources of consumer credit in Britain: finance companies, banks, credit cards, and stores.

A recent study by the Jubilee Centre in Cambridge which examined over a thousand people with debt problems showed them to owe these sources, on average, the following amounts of money:

Finance companies	£2,758
Banks	£1,789
Credit cards	£1,021
Stores	£ 725

As you can see, finance companies account for by far and away the largest amount of personal debt.

To a certain extent the figures are misleading. For one

thing, credit cards – like Access, Visa or Trustcard – are issued by banks. Also, although stores come fourth on the list, most store credit schemes are underwritten by independent finance companies (such as Curry's by Lombard Finance Ltd), and so a lot of the credit issued through shops has been counted under the first group instead of the fourth. Thirdly, people with store or credit card debts not infrequently 'pay them off' by taking out a single large loan from a finance company, thus transferring the debt to another source.

Of course money is owed to many other organisations too, among them building societies, insurance companies, mail order catalogues, British Gas, the electricity boards, and the Inland Revenue. In these cases, however, the amounts of money owed are smaller, and, with the exception of mail order catalogues, the services are not of a 'luxury' nature. You can do without a new car, but you can't do without fuel, and although you may feel like doing without Income Tax it is against the law to try!

By contrast, advertising by the 'big four' groups listed above deliberately draws attention to luxuries. What they're competing for is your 'surplus income' – the money left over on the end of the budget because it's not earmarked for anything else. Of course advertising for nearly all consumer goods, from Pepsi Cola to Land-Rovers, sets out to make the consumer spend disposable income instead of saving it. Credit advertising merely takes the job a stage further; it asks the consumer to spend his money, *even though in some cases it is money he hasn't yet earned*.

This confronts the advertiser with a problem.

In almost every case, borrowing money is expensive. Somebody buying a stereo system on credit will be paying back the asking price *plus* the interest. Naturally, if you ask the average shopper if he'd like to pay 10 or 20 per cent extra for his stereo, he'll say no – he wants the best deal he can get. So it's no good the advertiser going on about the cost. He must find other ways of recommending his offer.

Think about the picture the advertisements paint of you, the consumer. The credit advertiser does not see you as someone who wants to economise. That would be counterproductive. If you're thinking of using a credit facility, then according to the advertiser you must be after one of three things – *convenience*, *status*, or *handouts*.

Goodbye to the chequebook

Convenience is probably the commonest argument for buying on credit.

The ultimate convenience, of course, is the ability to buy goods you couldn't afford (or couldn't afford in large quantities) if you had to make a single payment. So credit can be presented as a kind of giveaway. The amounts vary, but if you walk down the average high street you are likely to see notices offering you anything from £200 to £2,000 to spend 'instantly'. No need to save up, no need to go without. The item you want can be yours right away.

Inside the store, glancing inside the pamphlets piled up by the cash register, you will find another argument brought forward. After all, the retailer is wasting his time giving you £300 of instant credit if there's nothing you want to buy. So the advertiser's next job is to tell you how much you want the goods the retailer is selling: not only is the three-piece suite or hi-fi an exceptionally good deal, it is the one you have always *dreamed of owning*. Banks can afford to cast the net a little wider, and accordingly emphasise the choice available to you by taking out a loan. You can take the furniture or hi-fi, but if you like you are perfectly free at the last moment to change your mind and go for a car, a boat, full double glazing or a holiday.

In their advertising material both retailers and banks have a tendency to resemble fairy godmothers. By

18

providing you with credit they are assisting you in the fulfilment of your dreams, rendering a generous and valuable service. This idea that credit-givers are doing you a favour is taken in other directions too. Storecard schemes that cover a group of retailers are apt to wax lyrical on the number of places where the card is accepted. Others point out that paying by account will relieve you of the apparently onerous responsibility of carrying a chequebook and cash.

Purchase by credit is more or less unanimously agreed among credit advertisers to be a vast improvement on previous forms of payment. Not only does it have an air of sophistication; it also allows you to plan your spending in advance and suppress irregularities in your cash-flow by (to use the vogue term) 'spreading the cost'. Typically the credit-giver undertakes to keep you informed, so that by the time next Saturday's spree comes along you know (to use another vogue term) how much 'spending power' is left in your account.

'Spending power' in fact means how much more you can buy from the shop before you owe them the maximum possible without going over your limit. Here's a simple but realistic example to show you how it works.

Assume that a store runs a continuous credit scheme, into which you pay £30 per month, and from which you are entitled to 'draw' goods to the value of £720 – twenty-four times your monthly repayment. If the interest on your credit (that is, on your debt) is charged at 2.4 per cent per month, the record of your transactions over four months might look like this:

Date:	Item:	Credit/Debit:	Balance:
Jan 1	Credit	£ 30.00	(cr) £ 30.00
Jan 4	Dresses	£ 89.90	

(continued)

19

Date:	Item:	Credit/Debit:	Balance:
Jan 27	Blouse	£ 21.95	
Feb 1	Credit	£ 30.00	(deb) £ 51.85
Feb 12	Lingerie	£ 27.90	
	Jewellery	£ 14.95	
	Shoes	£ 35.00	
Feb 23	Coat	£110.00	
Feb 28	Interest	£ 1.24	
Mar 1	Credit	£ 30.00	(deb) £159.09
Mar 16	Dress	£ 66.95	
	Skirt	£ 44.50	
	Tights	£ 3.00	
Mar 20	Blouse	£ 19.95	
Mar 31	Interest	£ 3.82	
Apr 1	Credit	£ 30.00	(deb) £257.31

There are two ways of looking at the situation on April 1. On the positive side, you are now dressed to kill and you still have an amazing £462.69 of 'spending power' left in your account. On the negative side, you have amassed a debt of £257.31 which, even if you buy nothing else from the store, will take you until Christmas to pay off at £30 per month. For the privilege of 'spreading the cost' over this extra three quarters of a year you will pay nearly £40 in interest.

It's worth adding a note here about charge cards. Charge card companies do not invite their customers to use their cards as a source of credit, and the financial penalties for doing so are severe (interest rates can rise as high as 3.5 per cent per month on outstanding debts). The conveniences, however, are much the same. Like credit cards, charge cards give you greater spending power and greater freedom from cash. What they don't do is impose a pre-set spending limit, and this is simultaneously an attraction for those whose incomes can support a charge card account, and a potential source of difficulty for those whose finances unexpectedly run aground.

Pride and perk factors

Association with wealth has made the charge card itself into something of a status symbol. This gives a company ample scope to heap praise, first on its services (for their efficiency and financial power), and second on its members (for having achieved a social position worthy of card ownership). You show your class not just by your Rolex watch, but by the method you use to pay for it.

The advertisers have tried hard to make some of the charge card status stick to credit cards and storecards. Consequently pamphlets remind you of the special treatment you will enjoy as a credit-user (which often means your name goes down on yet another mailing list), and that using the card does credit (so to speak) to your taste, judgement and intelligence.

Assured that opening an account is both sensible and convenient, however, there may still lurk in the mind of the canny customer a suspicion that he's being made to pay through the nose. To counter this the advertiser confronts the financial issue head on. Well, almost head on.

In some cases interest is reduced to zero (generally under a fixed-term repayment scheme for a single purchase); in others interest-free credit is offered as long as the outstanding balance is repaid within a given number of days. Further attractions are varied: price reductions on the first purchase, free entry into an exclusive prize draw, theatre tickets, cheap car hire, holidays, even free pens.

The most recent development is the promise of a handout not to the cardholder, but to charity. This commendable sentiment is, in some cases at least, borne out in practice – sums of money being donated in exchange for each new credit account opened. But while nobody wants to disparage charity giving, it's clear that the benefit runs both ways. A series of successful national fundraising events has proven beyond doubt that the British are willing to give large sums of money to a worthy cause. That being the case, worthy causes are inevitably thrown into the pool of ideas and images chosen by an advertiser to sell his product. The credit company probably also gains from the charity a large new mailing list to which it can send its advertising brochures.

There is something even more disturbing about this 'credit aid'. Credit advertising leads many families into trouble. Debt often results in marriage breakdown, divorce and child abuse. It is ironic that credit is sometimes advertised as assisting charity when in fact it is a contributing factor in many of the problems which charities seek to solve.

In the picture

Looked at closely, advertisements often look ridiculous. But you should be aware of the enormous power advertisements have, even while you're laughing at them. Partly this is because the advertiser is playing on some genuine desires; we really *do* like a convenient lifestyle; we *are* flattered by a boost to our status; and – let's be honest – none of us can resist a handout. In this way the advertiser's idea of 'who we are' isn't far from the truth.

But the advertisements work on another, more subtle level. Few advertisements today give you simple information – nearly always the words are accompanied by pictures. These pictures do not, as they once did, merely illustrate the product so that you know, for example, what a size 54 reinforced whalebone corset actually looks like.

Rather they provide a kind of background which, placed behind the product, makes the product more attractive. The rash of 1950s settings for jean and drink adverts is one example of this; another is the use of photographs in pamphlets advertising credit.

The 'background' in this case is usually a person, or a series of people, with whom the reader of the pamphlet is able to identify. For instance, there may be a thirtyish man posing with a twenty-fivish woman and two six or sevenish children. They are impeccably turned out, clearly well-off, and terribly, terribly happy. From such a picture the reader usually infers that he too (or she) can be like this with a little help from the credit scheme.

Consequently, the important question in credit advertising may not be 'Who do they think you are?' so much as 'Who do they think you'd like to be?' After all, as a typical British person you're unlikely to be content with yourself. The advertiser's skill is to make you believe, just for a moment, that his product can bridge the gap between the 'you' of the here and now and the 'you' of your dreams. The moment has to last long enough only for you to sign the cheque – or, in this case, the application form. That done, his job is complete.

Your self-image, then, is an important influence on the events that may eventually lead you to debt. It is also a key factor in sorting debt out, and escaping from it. But we'll explore that idea in another chapter. Next we're going to find out more about credit, and take a look behind the scenes at the companies who arrange it.

Chapter 3

Credit – A Look Behind the Scenes

There's something worth remembering about credit of all kinds:

The people who give credit don't give it for nothing.

That's one reason why credit is so easy to get. By granting you a personal loan the bank makes a profit on the interest you pay (as do the finance houses and moneylenders). By giving you a credit card, the bank gains through interest, but also takes a cut from the retailer's profit on your purchases. You may wonder why shops are so willing to let their customers use credit when the profit has to be shared. The answer is: the profit itself is bigger, since people paying on credit tend to buy more goods.

A second reason for the present credit boom is a change in the world economy, making the granting of personal credit a far more attractive option. But this needs a bit more explaining.

How things got to be the way they are

We're used to hearing about vast sums of money changing hands at the level of government and big business. It doesn't mean a lot to us because our own spending is done, at most, in hundreds and thousands, and not in millions. so there was something sobering in the news announced in May 1988 that, according to Government figures for March, the total amount of money owed by ordinary people in Britain (excluding mortgages) stood at over £37.9 *billion*.

Looking at credit as a commodity to be sold – on a par with training shoes or perfume – the rapid increase in demand since 1977 represents a huge success for the advertisers. After all, you've got to make people want something before they'll go out and buy it. But advertising isn't the only reason why credit has become more popular.

The advertisers have capitalised on changes that were occurring anyway. For example, the younger generation in Britain (who form the majority of debtors) attach far greater importance to material goods than their parents did. Fewer people today are content just to 'get by' or 'make do'. And the willingness of young people to go into debt to acquire things like hi-fi equipment and cars is increased by the longstanding social acceptability of borrowing to buy a house. If you're willing to take out a mortgage for £40,000, what's wrong with taking out a loan for £400?

And the organisations giving credit haven't only advertised – they've actually made it easier to borrow. Twenty years ago obtaining a loan involved an interview with the bank manager reminiscent of seeing the head at school. Now the banks are at pains to stress friendliness and informality. In fact once issued with a credit card you have an automatic right to borrow up to your credit limit with absolutely no questions asked.

Why the change? Before 1977 credit never used to be pushed the way it is now. And yet, to take one indicator, between 1982 and 1986 the amount of money spent on advertising credit cards on television and in the newspapers rose from £9.3 million to £16.7 million. No one invests that kind of money lightly, or without expecting a hefty return.

Three reasons for the credit boom

This is where we have to look briefly at the world economy. You could say that the credit boom has happened for three reasons:

1: It's profitable

In 1973 and 1978 two massive upheavals took place as a result of OPEC's decisions to raise the price of oil.

By charging high prices for their oil the producers made a great deal of money. Some of this they used to finance the modernisation of their own countries. But they also invested much of it abroad, not least in Britain. As a result the British banks suddenly had a lot of 'hot money', which they promptly invested by lending to the Third World. By the early eighties, however, it became clear that some Third World countries – especially in Africa and Latin America – were unable to repay their loans.

This international Debt Crisis had two results. One was that the movement of funds between the developed and the developing countries went into reverse, so that the net input of £30.4 billion to Third World economies in 1981 became a net outflow of £11 billion in 1983. The second result, following on this, was that the British banks started looking around for other places to invest their funds. Save for the effect of recession they might have put it into industry, but for various reasons industrial demand for loans was in decline. Consequently the banks turned to personal lending.

2: It's competitive

The credit boom is often blamed on the process of financial deregulation started by the Government in 1980. Since the rise in consumer debt can be traced back to 1977, deregulation can't be held responsible for starting the boom. What it did do was erase the lines of demarcation between various financial organisations. That's why many banks and building societies are now functioning also as stockbrokers, estate agents and providers of pensions. Of course many such services have no direct connection to credit. The point is that a customer attracted to a bank to obtain a loan may, for the sake of convenience, go to the same bank to take out an insurance policy. So credit is a selling point, part of the window dressing. And as the range of services on offer increases, so credit becomes more important as a means of attracting custom.

Credit is competitive also for the retailer. For one thing, if he can persuade a customer to open a store account he will almost automatically ensure that the customer buys more goods from the store. But more important than that, he will get a free profile of the customer's spending habits, and so increase the efficiency and effectiveness of his mail-shots, store organisation, and advertising.

3: It's possible

That may sound peculiar until you realise that the system of instant credit depends on some highly sophisticated technology.

Credit cards and automatic overdraft facilities are highly economical in comparison to the old method of individual, personal assessment for every loan. What used to be done by men and women is now done by computers, and done a lot faster and a lot more cheaply. Since producing the same level of service without automation would be astronomically expensive, the new technology has actually reduced the cost of lending and, indirectly, the cost of borrowing.

At the same time automation deprives the credit system of humanity. There may be some reassurance in getting a loan without having to explain why you need the cash, but when the form letters arrive demanding repayment, you are liable to feel you're not dealing with human beings at all, only a machine.

Those are some of the reasons behind the growth of the credit industry at what might be called the 'top end of the market'.

The relationship between the banks and the finance companies that account for the largest slice of consumer debt is complex. Each of the so-called Big Four clearing banks has a finance company of its own (for instance Barclays own Mercantile Credit, and Midland own Forward Trust). Some finance companies, like Ford Motor Credit Company Ltd, are linked to major retailers or manufacturers. Others have no direct connection, but raise the money they lend by dealing on the financial markets or borrowing from banks.

To the ordinary consumer this matters little. What does matter is the terms on which credit is offered 'on the street'.

Chapter 4

The Connoisseur's Credit Guide

Never sign a bad deal

The perks used by the advertisers to recommend one brand of credit over another sometimes make it hard to know which is best. So if you're thinking of borrowing money, or paying for goods with a storecard, work from this simple guideline:

Never sign a bad deal.

Obvious?

Well, not as obvious as you'd think. There are all kinds of reasons why people sign – literally or metaphorically – the worst deals imaginable. Because they think it's the best they can get. Because they can't be bothered to look for anything better. Because they feel intimidated. Because they're desperate.

In every case, of course, the short term benefits seem to outweigh the long term costs. What's two pounds a week when you can get a microwave oven right now? Or, what does it matter that you're taking on another debt, if only you can get your present debts cleared? In some cases people can be in such dire straits that they'll go to a

31

moneylender fully knowing they have no prospect of paying back the loan. In the words of one debtor: 'You get to the stage when one of these fellows knocks on the door, says you can have two hundred quid, and even though you've got to pay eight hundred back, you're so desperate you'll still snap his arm off to get it.'

A person who borrows on terms like that isn't doing himself any favours. He might as well try armed robbery for all the good it'll do him in the long run! No matter how urgent the need, *never sign a bad deal*.

All right. But how do you distinguish a bad deal from a good one?

Here you need to consider two things. The first is how much the credit costs. The second is the risk involved in obtaining it. We'll look at both of these in more detail.

APRs and all that

If you had to pay back exactly the sum you borrowed, using credit would present few problems. But borrowing is expensive. You nearly always pay interest, and sometimes other charges as well.

Since rates of interest vary widely, it is essential to shop around. Here Government legislation is very useful, because all organisations offering credit are required by law to state the total amount they charge. The figure to look for is called the APR – the Annual Percentage Rate of interest. Calculating the APR can be hard; that doesn't matter – the lender should calculate it for you, and if he doesn't then you shouldn't be borrowing from him.

The APR is useful because, like the price per kilo in a greengrocer's, it enables you to compare one offer with another. The general rule is:

The higher the APR:
the higher the interest,
the worse the deal.

Don't forget, though, that the effect of the APR will vary according to the length of the repayment period. Look at DIAGRAM 1. The information on this is taken from a real finance company advertisement, where it is entitled 'GENUINE LOW CALENDAR MONTHLY REPAYMENTS'. What the advertisement tells you is how much you have to repay, over what length of time, and at what APR. DIAGRAM 1 shows you what this means in terms of *actual money laid out*.

For a start, you can see that *proportionally* the borrower pays less for £12,000 than he does for £2,000. In other words the company is following standard practice by charging a lower rate of interest for larger loans. But look at how the cost of that interest rate increases with the repayment period. Paid back over three years, a loan of £2,000 costs the borrower an extra £491.20. Paid back over fifteen years, it costs him an extra £3,000.40 – in other words he pays two and a half times more than the amount he borrowed.

Of course it's easier to pay back the loan over fiteen years at £27.78 a month than over three years at £69.22. That's the attraction of 'spreading the cost'. Still, bear it in mind that:

Paying back quickly costs less.

This kind of loan is referred to as *fixed-term credit*. That

33

is because you're told before you make the agreement what the repayments are going to be (roughly, because the APR will vary slightly), and when they're due. Examples of fixed-term credit include: personal bank loans, mortgages, and some shop credit accounts.

The word 'credit', however, is more often associated with a different way of charging interest, called *revolving credit*. Most store cards and all bank credit cards offer revolving credit. So too do the charge cards, in the event of the cardholder defaulting on repayment. Individual cards vary in the terms they offer, but generally the user is given a pre-set spending limit, and interest is charged at the end of each month on whatever credit is outstanding in the account.

An example of revolving credit, was given in Chapter 2. The problem with revolving credit is that the interest charged at the end of one month increases the amount on which interest is due at the end of the next. Assume, for instance, that a customer has used £200 of credit on an account where interest is charged at 2.45 per cent per month (APR = 33.7 per cent). If he makes no further purchases, and defaults on his repayments, then over twelve months his debt will increase as follows:

Month:	Interest paid:	Balance now owed by borrower:
Jan	£4.90	£204.90
Feb	£5.02	£209.92
Mar	£5.14	£215.06
Apr	£5.27	£220.33
May	£5.40	£225.73
Jun	£5.53	£231.26
Jul	£5.67	£236.93
Aug	£5.80	£242.73

(continued)

Month:	Interest paid:	Balance now owed by borrower:
Sep	£5.95	£248.68
Oct	£6.09	£254.77
Nov	£6.24	£261.01
Dec	£6.39	£267.40

In other words, at the end of the year he owes over £60 more than he did at the beginning – simply because of the interest.

Finance companies issuing cards try to prevent default by setting a fixed, or minimum, monthly repayment. This may be £5, £10, or perhaps 1/24th of the spending limit. In the example from which the above figures were taken the smallest amount the cardholder can pay back each month is £5. But if he had paid £5 in January instead of defaulting, it would have made little impact on the debt, since £5 only just covered the £4.90 he owed in interest. At the end of January he would have reduced the amount he owed by exactly 10p!

This is what makes revolving credit so dangerous. In fact in numerous cases the amount owed is so large that it grows through interest even as it's being repaid. The cardholder takes one step forward, and two steps back. As a result, with revolving credit agreements the comparison of APRs is particularly important. They vary a lot. An informal survey of high street credit facilities on offer in Edinburgh in 1988 produced the following results:

Company:	APRs: *
Currys	41.7 (33.7)
Laskys (Gold Card)	39.9 (33.7)
Dixons	38.4 (33.7)

(continued)

Company:	APRs:*
Sears	34.4 (34.4)
Dorothy Perkins	34.4 (32.1)
Top Man (Budget Account)	34.4 (32.1)
Debenhams	34.4 (26.8)
Dorothy Perkins (Option Account)	34.4 (26.8)
BHS (Storecard)	32.9 (29.0)
Littlewoods	32.5 (28.5)
Laura Ashley	32.1 (26.8)
C&A	32.1 (27.5)
Marks and Spencer (Budgetcard and Chargecard)	29.8 (29.8)
Next (Option Account)	29.8 (29.8)
Top Man (Option Account)	– (26.8)
Ratners	0.00 (0.00)
Samuel	0.00 (0.00)

* For payment by cheque or Giro. Figure for payment by direct debit/standing order is given in brackets. Data gathered from advertising material available in December 1988.

The shops in the table are ranked according to the APR charged if you pay by cheque or giro. That the figures are high is owing in part to the credit companies' fear of borrower default. The theory is that a customer who has to write out a cheque every month represents a higher risk than the one who pays by direct debit. Consequently most credit schemes offer a lower APR to direct debit borrowers, and these figures are given above in brackets.

With the help of a table like this you might think that finding a good credit deal is straightforward. But there can be hidden snags. So finally, here are some hints on working out the cost of credit:

1: Prices

It's easy to forget when you're comparing the cost of credit agreements that a shop offering cheap or zero interest may be charging you more for the goods you want to buy. This is often the case with cars. What you need to keep in mind is that good deals are not created by magic. At the end of the day the retailer has to balance his books, and if he's offering you zero percent interest he must have some other method of retrieving the cash. It may be that the reduction is genuine, and that he plans to make his profit through a boost in sales. It may not. At any rate, you can find out what the deal's worth by calculating the savings on interest and adding them to the deal's worth by adding on the missing interest and comparing the result with the cost of the same goods offered under conventional credit terms. If it's higher, you'll be paying for the zero interest out of your own pocket.

2: Extra charges

The APR will tell you how much your credit is going to cost you. But it may not tell you about other, related expenses. For example, a bank overdraft, regarded as one of the cheapest forms of loan, will usually result in your being charged for bank services – like the processing of cheques – that otherwise are provided free. This must be considered alongside the APR.

3: Further help

This book does not go into detail on all the forms of credit available. If you want more information on using credit or handling a debt crisis, it is advisable to get professional and confidential advice (see Appendix 2 at the back of this book). There are also other books available which go into details on all *aspects of debt management. We recommend Ann Andrew's and Peter Houghton's* How to Cope with Credit and Deal with Debt.

The risks of credit

The main risk associated with using credit arises from the nature of credit itself.

In signing a credit agreement you are committing yourself to pay off a debt with money you have not yet earned. To use the words of the old proverb, you are having to count your chickens before they're hatched – a dicey business when the unemployment rate is in the millions. Of course no one wants to live in constant fear of disaster. But you have to be realistic. People *do* get made redundant; they *do* unexpectedly fall ill; they *do* find themselves faced with sudden, uninsured expenses. And if they have taken on credit agreements these circumstances frequently push them into debt.

So think carefully before you use credit. Ask yourself:

Am I sure I'll be able to afford the repayments?

Particularly bear in mind what you read in the last section about the cost of credit, and the effect of your repayment rate on the total amount you pay. To obtain '£300 Instant Credit' you could easily be committing over £400 of your future income. If you take credit from a local moneylender or tallyman you will almost certainly face an APR of more than 60 per cent, and possibly – in the worst cases – up to 1,000 per cent.

Figures like that indicate how unwise it is to obtain credit on the doorstep. But this kind of borrowing is unwise for another reason too. If for any reason you are unable to pay the lender there is no way of stopping the debt growing, often at an alarming rate.

By contrast, you will see in much of the advertising put out by stores, banks and finance companies a section with a heading like 'Peace of Mind'. It means that the broker is offering insurance along with the credit, so that repayments are not interrupted in the event of your being laid off or taken ill. Insurance is generally added to the monthly repayment – with a NatWest personal loan of £500, for instance, the total extra cost of insurance over two years is £25.

As a rule of thumb:

If you can insure your credit, do so.

But remember to check exactly what it is you will be insured against, and how long the insurance cover lasts. The more eventualities are mentioned in the policy document ('accident', 'sickness', 'redundancy', 'unemployment'), the more peace of mind you can have that your payments will be covered. Also, insurance companies always go by the letter of an agreement, not by the spirit. Never hurry when you fill in the form, because if you omit to mention, say, a past illness, the company may claim that you withheld information from them, and refuse to pay up.

Finally, for home owners, here are two more key areas of risk in the use of credit:

1: Secured loans

A national daily newspaper recently carried a box ad for personal loans which outlined the terms and advantages offered,

39

and invited the reader to phone immediately a London number displayed at the bottom. Beneath the number and the company address, in letters about half a millimetre high and actually set in to the line surrounding the advertisement, were these words: *LOANS SECURED ON PROPERTY*.

The difference between secured and unsecured credit is important. Storecards and bank credit cards offer unsecured credit: in other words, the lender is relying solely on your future income to retrieve what is owed. If you default, and are heavily in debt, he may never see the money again. In view of this, finance companies offering loans nearly always demand that you put up your house (or sometimes an insurance policy) as security.

In effect, by taking out a loan secured on property you are giving the finance company a legal right to take your home away if you default. Building societies, in particular, are very unwilling to do this. But make no mistake; when all other options have been closed off even a building society will observe the letter of the law. Most agreements permit a company to call in the whole loan if you miss just a single payment. Failure to return the money you've borrowed within a specified period (usually four weeks) entitles the company to go to court and ask for possession of your house. Twenty thousand cases of house possession by building societies, banks and finance companies were recorded in 1987 alone.

The moral: don't take out secured loans unless you're either; (1) certain of being able to repay, or (2) willing to lose your home.

2: Equity release

On the face of it, equity release is a brand new way of borrowing money.

One newspaper advertisement puts it like this: 'DEAR HOME OWNER, Why not "UNLOCK SOME OR ALL OF THE PROFIT" that you have already made on your home and make the most of your greatest investment?'

How does equity release work? Well, as anyone who has

bought a house will know, a large slice of your income goes to pay off the mortgage. This can leave you short of ready cash, but gradually increases the 'equity' (the part of the mortgage you have already paid) on your home. A property worth £80,000, with a £30,000 outstanding mortgage, has an equity value of £50,000.

Equity release allows the home owner to borrow up to the equity value of his home, thus 'freeing' his 'locked-up' capital. It differs little from a second mortgage; both are loans, and both are secured on property. So the money the borrower releases is not, as the advertisement suggests, a personal investment he could not otherwise get at. It comes from the bank or the finance company, and using it to the full simply puts him back where he was when he took out the mortgage – owing the entire value of his house.

In fact the situation is worse, for two reasons. One, the APR on equity release is almost always higher than that on the original mortgage. And two, unlike a house, the kind of things the 'released' capital is used to pay for almost always decrease in value. After twenty years a house can usually be sold for a tidy profit; a car will long since have turned into a heap of rust.

Chapter 5

Never Happen to Me?

We've seen already that a state of chronic debt can be reached in a number of different ways.

The circumstances leading to debt aren't necessarily the fault of the debtor. For example, a woman abandoned by her husband or partner, and having small children to support, may be put under such intense pressure financially that debt becomes almost inevitable. The same can happen with unexpected pregnancies, bereavement, and failures in business.

In the end, successful money management is about balancing the books – making sure you're earning at least as much as you're laying out. The charts in DIAGRAM 2 show three reasons why this may not occur. You'll see that each chart illustrates a relationship between income, living expenses, and credit repayments. What's left after you've deducted essential living expenses from income is usually called your 'surplus income' – money you don't have to spend if you don't want to. It is this money you are using when you take out a credit agreement, for a house, a car, or a video machine, and if you want your books to balance these credit repayments must be covered by the surplus.

Three ways into debt

One way into debt trouble – A – is simply to let your borrowing get out of hand. This often happens through inattention to the real cost of credit, especially when earnings are low. It's worth bearing in mind that, according to recent research, people with a weekly income of less than £100 have, on average, a surplus of only £1. Those who earn between £100 and £200 have £16; those earning over £200 have £44.

Most readers of this book will know how their living expenses vary from month to month. But there are some times when you are particularly hard hit (for instance when a couple of large fuel bills arrive), and some changes of circumstance, like a pregnancy or an increase in the mortgage rate, that will make a permanent impact on your spending. This increase in living expenses – B – has the same effect as an increase in credit repayments, narrowing the gap between outlay and income.

The third way into debt – C – involves a loss of earnings. This doesn't always imply redundancy. Critical falls in income also follow cuts in overtime, withdrawal of child benefit, illness, divorce, and, for the self-employed, failure in business. Of the three ways into debt, C is generally the most drastic. It is also the most common.

By and large the events that lead to serious debt are not catastrophes on a grand scale. They are what we call the 'ups and downs' of everyday life, and they only become dangerous when you keep your spending too close to your income. If your spending breaks through your income on a regular basis, like rocks in a shallow stream, it won't take much to dry up your cash-flow completely. One hard winter, one uninsured car accident, one unexpected addition to the family, and you're in the red.

Really we are saying again that in the majority of cases serious debt is reached by living on the knife-edge, living beyond your means.

The man in debt today is the same one who yesterday insisted he was 'creditworthy', 'able to meet his commitments', 'financially secure'. But when he said 'I'll

44

never be in debt', he really meant, 'I've never been in debt before'. Ironically, his very self-confidence (an attitude encouraged by the advertisers) contributed to his downfall. He simply wouldn't believe he had a debt problem until he'd taken several decisive steps into trouble.

Lack of foresight can be blamed for a good many disastrous situations. Of course, not everyone in debt has lacked foresight in the same way or the the same degree, nor have they reached their present state in ways quite as simple as the ones suggested in DIAGRAM 2. Reality is always complicated. A person who is now firmly in debt has probably lived on the fringes of debt for years; he may have been in debt trouble before, got out of it, gone back in. He may be owing money in so many directions he can barely remember who his creditors are.

To give an idea of this complexity we're going to look at another example. The information does not come from any single case history; the couple described do not actually exist, and their stituation has been deliberately constructed to show clearly how the slide into debt might begin. Of course it is still simpler than reality. But not much simpler.

This could be you.

A debt story

Richard and Michelle are an ordinary couple, with ordinary means, and ordinary hopes and expectations. They are in their late twenties, and have two children who are old enough to go to school, thus freeing Michelle to take a part-time job. The children are more of a burden financially now than their parents anticipated: the grocery bill is bigger than it used to be, Christmas is more expensive, and now that the children are at school there are new clothes and school outings to be paid for.

45

Nonetheless Michelle's return to work has given the family a bit more leeway, and they now have enough spare cash to raise a mortgage and buy their first house. As you can see from the balance sheet for April, below, they pay back £230.00 (net) every month on the mortgage, of which £26,480.00 remains outstanding. Their other main financial commitment is a bank loan, taken out a month before in order to replace a dodgy old car. With the children at school the family needs its own transport more than ever, and having had so much trouble with the previous vehicle Richard felt it was worthwhile stretching the budget to buy the next one brand new. As a result they now owe the bank £4527.98, which they are paying back in monthly instalments of £96.34.

Richard and Michelle's combined net monthly income (that is, after tax and superannuation have been deducted) is £845.00, and this covers their two main credit commitments, as well as the day to day living expenses listed under 'cash and cheques' – usually the largest single item on their monthly expenses. Richard does not keep a close eye on his bank account – certainly he would never write down the figures as they are written down here – but he is aware that he has less money than he did before he started paying for his house and his car, and when the monthly statements come in from his three credit accounts (a bank credit card, a storecard, and a store budget account with fixed monthly repayments), he always sends a cheque promptly to avoid incurring interest. The balance sheet for April shows that he has paid back £50.25 and £32.00 respectively on his credit card and storecard. Only on his budget account does he 'spread the cost' by paying less than the total due:

Year One April	Month's income:	Month's outlay:	Remaining bank bal.:	Spending on credit:	Remaining debt:
Richard:	620.00				
Michelle:	225.00				
Mortgage:		230.00			(26,480.00)
Bank loan:		96.34			4,527.98
Cash/cheques:		356.50			
Credit card:		50.25		72.00	72.00
Storecard:		32.00			
Budgetcard:		20.00			143.76
TOTAL:	845.00	794.09	223.31	72.00	4,743.74

In the short term at least, Richard and Michelle's financial situation looks fairly healthy. Their total remaining debt (given here excluding the mortgage) is gradually going down. By the end of the month they have earned more than they've spent, as a result of which the remaining bank balance has slightly increased from the £172.40 they had at the end of the previous month. This would not have been the case had they made the additional purchase of £72.00 with cash or cheques, but since they used the credit card the cost is pushed forward into May.

In May Richard and Michelle pay back the £72.00, then spend a further £15.00 using the credit card, and £19.00 using the storecard. Since their income does not vary, and their general spending in cash and cheques is down slightly on the previous month, the remaining bank balance again increases:

Year One May	Month's income:	Month's outlay:	Remaining bank bal.:	Spending on credit:	Remaining debt:
Richard:	620.00				
Michelle:	225.00				
Mortgage:		230.00			(26,250.00)
Bank loan:		96.34			4,431.64
Cash/cheques:		342.00			

(continued)

Year One May	Month's income:	Month's outlay:	Remaining bank bal.:	Spending on credit:	Remaining debt:
Credit card:		72.00		15.00	15.00
Storecard:				19.00	19.00
Budgetcard:		20.00			126.77
TOTAL:	845.00	760.34	307.97	34.00	4,592.41

June, however, sees the arrival of the quarterly gas and electricity bills. Since Richard pays both of these by cheque, their expenses for June are greater than their income, and the remaining balance goes down to £239.43:

Year One June	Month's income:	Month's outlay:	Remaining bank bal.:	Spending on credit:	Remaining debt:
Richard:	620.00				
Michelle:	225.00				
Mortgage:		230.00			(26,020.00)
Bank loan:		96.34			4,335.30
Cash/cheques:		533.20			
Credit card:		15.00		140.00	140.00
Storecard:		19.00			
Budgetcard:		20.00			109.28
TOTAL:	845.00	913.54	239.43	140.00	4,814.48

Note something else about the June balance sheet.

When he bought a car Richard promised himself that they would forgo a summer holiday this year. But the children are disappointed, and so at the last minute he changes his mind and books a week in Devon. He calculates that the £140.00 spent on accommodation will double by the time he's paid for travel and meals out. Because he can't pay this out of savings, he uses his credit card, planning to spread the total cost in monthly repayments of £25.00

At first the plan seems to work. His prediction of the holiday costs is more or less correct, and in spite of another round of bills in September, by October his remaining bank

balance stands at £375.37 – the highest that year. But in the
first week of October he gets bad news: in an effort to
compete his firm is streamlining its workforce, and he is to
be made redundant with a month's notice.

Consequently, the balance sheet for November looks
like this:

Year One November	Month's income:	Month's outlay:	Remaining bank bal.:	Spending on credit:	Remaining debt:
Richard:	1,772.30				
Michelle:	225.00				
Mortgage:		230.00			(24,870.00)
Bank loan:		96.34			3,853.36
Cash/cheques:		320.00			
Credit card:		10.00			180.69
Storecard:		10.00			57.43
Budgetcard:		20.00			26.68
TOTAL:	1,997.30	686.34	1,686.33		4,164.23

The massive addition to Richard's income for this month
is made by a redundancy payment of £1630.00 – his weekly
wage (to a maximum of £163.00) multiplied by the number
of years he has been at the firm. Basically, however, his
financial outlook is gloomy: he's now claiming unemployment benefit, which leaves Michelle as the main earner
on just £225.00. They make some small economies,
including a reduction in their credit repayments to £10.00
on the credit card and storecard, but not surprisingly,
for the first time this year, the month's outlay heavily
outweighs the month's income.

Richard's state of mind here is crucial. He has never
been out of work before, and he is certain it won't be
long before he finds another position. This accounts for
the fact that when December comes along he uses his credit
card to give the family the sort of Christmas they've been
used to:

Year One December	Month's income:	Month's outlay:	Remaining bank bal.:	Spending on credit:	Remaining debt:
Richard:	142.30				
Michelle:	225.00				
Mortgage:		230.00			(24,640.00)
Bank loan:		96.34			3,757.26
Cash/cheques:		458.00			
Credit card:		10.00		120.40	296.18
Storecard:		10.00		25.00	48.38
Budgetcard:		20.00			6.84
TOTAL:	367.30	824.34	1,229.29	145.40	4,108.66

During the first two months of the following year the redundancy payment picks up the slack from Richard's loss of income. It isn't until March that he acknowledges his unemployment may last longer than expected, and takes a part-time job behind a bar in the evenings. By now, though, he is in real trouble:

Year Two March	Month's income:	Month's outlay:	Remaining bank bal.:	Spending on credit:	Remaining debt:
Richard:	177.30				
Michelle:	225.00				
Mortgage:		254.00			(23,950.00)
Bank loan:		96.34			3,468.24
Cash/cheques:		758.90			
Credit card:		10.00			280.94
Storecard:		10.00			35.73
Budgetcard:		20.00			4.67
TOTAL:	402.30	1,149.24	− 181.37		3,789.58

The problem is borne in on him by a combination of expenses, for in March not only does he have to pay the fuel bills and buy the children badly needed new clothes, but the road tax and insurance are due on the car. The outlay of £758.90 effectively wipes out what remains of his redundancy money. On top of all that, the building society has increased its mortgage lending rate, with the result that Richard now has to pay £254.00 per month instead of £230.00. At £10.00 per month he is making slow headway against his credit card debt, and there is a serious possibility he may not be able to sustain the mortgage.

The additional £35.00 per month brought in by his pub work cannot prevent the balance sliding further into the red at the end of April. This stings him into further action, though not of the wisest sort. In an effort to reduce his spending in cash and cheques, he borrows £115.00 from his credit card account, and uses his storecard to pay for some goods he would normally have bought elsewhere.

At the end of May he has knocked his spending in cash and cheques down to £72.00. But he has now almost reached his £400.00 spending limit on the credit card, and the bank balance has slumped to £ – 434.52:

Year Two May	Month's income:	Month's outlay:	Remaining bank bal.:	Spending on credit:	Remaining debt:
Richard:	177.30				
Michelle:	225.00				
Mortgage:		254.00			(23,410.00)
Bank loan:		96.34			3,275.56
Cash/cheques:		72.00			
Credit card:		5.00		115.00	396.56
Storecard:		5.00		78.99	104.23
Budgetcard:				29.90	29.90
Bank charges:					4.28
TOTAL:	402.30	432.34	– 434.52	223.89	3,810.53

With the prospect of another round of fuel bills in June, Richard decides it is time to go to the bank manager and come clean.

Much to his relief he is offered an overdraft facility of £2,000.00. This feels to him rather like a second redundancy payment, as though he now has more to spend. In fact nothing could be further from the truth. The overdraft does not show up on the balance sheet for June as a sum of money injected into his account. The term 'remaining bank balance' now has little meaning, because until further notice he is in a state of permanent debt to the bank:

Year Two June	Month's income:	Month's outlay:	Remaining bank bal.:	Spending on credit:	Remaining debt:
Richard:	177.30				
Michelle:	225.00				
Mortgage:		254.00			(23,640.00)
Bank loan:		96.34			3,179.22
Cash/cheques:		481.80			
Credit card:		5.00			399.49
Storecard:		5.00			101.84
Budgetcard:		20.00		5.50	4.67
Overdraft:					894.36
Bank charges:					8.68
TOTAL:	402.30	862.14	00.00	5.50	4,598.52

Richard and Michelle's progress over the last fifteen months can be seen on DIAGRAM 3. The chart shows how precarious their finances were, even at the beginning; every time the fuel bills came round their expenses exceeded their income, and now that their income's been halved there's no way they can support both themselves and their debts.

Richard's decision to use an overdraft is understandable. But it's hard to see how it's going to help him. He might

52

say that it buys him time. But time to do what? If he hasn't been able to find work for seven months, is he right to gamble on finding it in four? Four months is all the time he's got. In four months (assuming he doesn't use the overdraft to pay off his credit and storecard debts) he will have used up most of the £2,000.00; his total outstanding debt will have leapt back up to over £5,000.00 – far more than he owed in April of the previous year; and his debt to the credit company, now being paid back at the minimum £5.00 per month, will actually have increased.

At that point, Richard – still with his new car, still living in his own house and appearing to be a successful young man – will start to ponder his options. Being the person he is, probably he will not stoop to opening a new storecard account merely for the purpose of cashing the instant credit. He could go back to the bank manager and extend his overdraft. But might he be refused? A finance company might be less inquisitive of his ability to repay, and after all, he would have the house to put up as security . . .

In the long run, none of these solutions will help him. Every new loan, every 'breathing space' he gets, only forces him to carry a weightier burden of repayments in the future. And that future may not be brightened by the landing of a well-paid job, as he hopes. It could be that Richard and Michelle will have to reconcile their present financial troubles to a lifetime of relative poverty, with Richard employed at a wage that can hardly sustain a mortgage, still less their accumulated debts. In short, they will begin to experience the darker side of the credit boom.

It's pretty unpleasant.

Chapter 6

Life on the Inside

Default – and what comes after

Debt problems begin to bite the moment you first default.

You may not notice. Until then, whatever your problems, you will have been treated by your creditors as a sound and reliable customer, and you will probably have regarded yourself the same way. Defaulting, though, sets off a chain reaction in your status. Soon the creditor's letter isn't just a friendly reminder; it's a default notice. You have broken the terms of the agreement by failing to pay the due amount on the due date, and he wants you to pay up.

This is understandable – after all, if he's a respectable dealer he'll have informed you of the conditions of credit, and will take your signature as proof that you agree to them and mean to comply. More than that, he will probably be mindful of the threat posed to his profitability and competitiveness, and the need to prevent credit users in general defaulting with impunity because they think they can get away with it.

For these reasons default is treated seriously, and communications from the creditor take on an ominous tone.

The default notice itself notifies you that the agreement is to be terminated, usually in seven days. On termination the creditor is entitled to demand full payment of the outstanding debt, and to start charging 'default interest' on whatever you fail to repay. Depending on the type of agreement, he may also be entitled to repossess his goods (if you have bought them on hire-purchase) or enforce security (if you have taken out a secured loan).

If you fail to respond to a default notice the creditor is left in an awkward position.

He can compel you to pay only by taking you to court. But this is risky. Court actions are long and involved, and not infrequently settled on terms favourable to the debtor. Unless his loan was secured, therefore, the creditor is likely to see prosecution as a last resort. Instead, he will probably now start a campaign of intimidation. He will *threaten* you with court action, in the hope that this will scare you into paying him before you pay your other creditors. He will send a series of computer-written letters, or start to telephone you. If he is a local moneylender or a tallyman he will confront you on the doorstep, perhaps even in the street.

This stage begins about two months after default. At some point in those two months, you, the debtor, now perhaps in the habit of stuffing the dreaded window-envelopes unopened into a drawer, are forced to face up to the situation. Possibly the man arrives to disconnect the gas, or you get a midnight phone call from the finance company. At any rate, you start opening the envelopes, and discover to your horror that you have three court actions pending, and a fistful of debts that are already hopeless and getting bigger by the month.

Side effects of debt

The anguish produced by all this is hard to imagine for anyone who has not been in debt himself. Debt is rarely a private problem. It is an affliction of whole households, a destroyer of families. That, in fact, is the major reason why debt is turning into a national crisis. It's impossible to know how many are suffering directly or indirectly as a result of debt. But considering the fact that most debtors are married or have children, and that every year more then two million debt cases reach the county courts, the number must be pretty large.

The nightmare of debt is made worse by the fact that less scrupulous creditors will sometimes back up their demands with harassment and threats of physical violence – methods strictly prohibited under the Administration of Justice Act 1970, but often not reported by debtors for fear of recrimination. It's hardly surprising, therefore, that debt – like cancer or bereavement – has side-effects.

Chronic debt is like losing a loved one – it's an experience lots of people have, and it's an experience that affects most people in the same way. Of course no two situations are identical. But speak to somebody with debt problems and he, or she, will almost always tell you about feelings of guilt, anger, fear, shame, loss of confidence, loss of dignity, loss of hope. These things make up the landscape of debt.

That may seem a bit depressing. But knowing about it does have one big advantage – it proves you're not alone. If you are suffering the side-effects of debt, you can be sure that hundreds of thousands of people in Britain are feeling just the same as you are. Here are the comments some of them have made:

1: Moira Paget, on anxiety:

'Daily it does unconsciously grind away at you. Girls I went to school with who are leading different lives from me now are much more haunted by debt, they say it is part of their lot. I dare say every other one is in debt of some kind. I think a lot of time and anxiousness is taken up dealing with it. If someone comes to the door you think: I'll pay

57

him, but I'll have to leave the woman who brings the vegetables on Friday. And so you're continually balancing it out. You can't pay everybody.'

2: Jean Betts, on children:

'You feel as if you're letting the children down because you can't afford to buy everything. The television tells you to buy the children this and that, and the children say I want. I know I've gone through pockets and money banks to get enough money for food and things like that.'

3: Ian Mackie, on social life

'It's a very stressful time. The marriage is often on the verge of breaking up. I discussed finances with my wife, but the fact is you can't do so many things. You can't go out for a pint, you can't go out for a meal, we don't smoke, we don't drink much. We cannot have a social life, can we? I cannot get a job that will pay the rent and leave anything left to live on. My wife cannot get back to work because we would lose the dole money. It's Catch-22. If you could both work it would be different.'

4: Sue Emery, on harassment:

'A while back they would just keep writing and phoning, and they phoned at the most ridiculous times, nine, ten in the evening, and they were quite hostile sometimes, you know, saying: Why have you got yourself into this mess? And I always said: I've had a baby. And they say: Yes, and what else? I say: Well, that's it, I've had a baby. I mean some people just don't realise how much babies cost. I mean we haven't got anything new for Michael – everything is secondhand. But still they think, Oh, this person's just mucking about . . .'

5: Ann Hunter, on fear:

'Every time someone came to the door we were terrified of the bailiffs because we owed money left right and centre. Our biggest fear was that the bailiffs would come while the children were there. To me that was the end of the world. Never having been in that situation before, with two children, I was petrified. My husband and I were both very much on edge. The children must have suffered a lot. In the end we got this council flat. Our neighbours next door gave us the carpets and a friend came and helped us to do up the flat. It was in a real state. It's a point where you lose all your pride.'

6: Irene Bancroft, on lying:

'Some women get into debt and don't tell their husbands. They'll produce things and they say: I bought this for fifty pence from Marjorie down the street. And in truth it cost fifty pounds and they're still paying the club man. And if their husband's the old fashioned type he gives her X pounds a weeks to pay the bills. Women always think they need things, not generally for themselves but for the house and children. Then it gets to the stage when they can't face it . . .'

7: Sandra Day, on self-image:

'I know it's not major, but the washing machine has broken, and the hoover, and I can't afford to get them repaired. The day to day running of the house is suffering. My hair needs cutting, as you've probably noticed, but I just can't afford it. Most of the time I just feel a mess, you know, and then my confidence comes down. I feel everybody is looking at me and thinking I don't look smart. My work is suffering, too, and I'm forgetting silly little things, like to defrost the chicken for Wednesday's dinner. I'm fairly organised, but all this is getting worse.'

8: *Mary Wilson, on illness:*

'I suffered. I used to lie in bed at night and cry myself to sleep, thinking what on earth can I do, as I hadn't got a mother or father or anything like that, you see. I went down and down. I hardly ate anything because I was worried. My main job was to feed the children and I used to eat what they left, and my health suffered. I never went anywhere. We had one holiday which the Catholic church paid for. My husband was an alcoholic and I had to keep it quiet, even when he used to beat me up. When I ended up in hospital I wouldn't tell anybody. I think I went down to four stone two. I was just skin and bone.'

9: *John Scott, on suicide:*

'When I found my wife unconscious, it really shocked me. I hadn't really been sharing with her. I'm not particularly worried about the money, I'd always pay it back. I was more concerned for my wife's welfare. They kept pestering her. I think it was mainly debt collection agencies, and people ringing me up. I hadn't got a clue who they were. I had no inkling that we were in financial trouble, she'd kept it all to herself, and that's why she was in that state. She'd taken an overdose, and it wasn't a cry for help, it was a serious attempt.'

10: *Peter Schilner, on family:*

'Friends and family don't really understand. It has been dragging on for so long they are fed up with it. Pat says she is not very hungry and does not eat any of the food that is put on the table at mealtimes. Bit by bit friends didn't come any more. The relatives still came, but they did not understand. They kept telling us to get ourselves out of this state, but we couldn't until we got a proper job.'

11: Pat Schilner, the last word:

'The twelve year old child realises quite a bit, and says: Why do you and Dad fight so much, you are not going to get divorced or split up, are you? The younger child, one day when things were truly bad, said: Look Mum, take the money from my piggybank . . .'

Debt is miserable.

Ironically, what lies at the end of the road so dazzlingly illuminated by the credit advertisers is a lifestyle as different from the one you were promised as black is different from white. Credit is offered to you as a means of enjoying life's luxuries – in the words of the hackneyed sales pitch, of taking the waiting out of wanting. But for hundreds of thousands of buyers whose good credit is disintegrating into bad debt, those luxuries will be like a passing dream. The furniture will be taken back, the new car sold, the hard-won first home repossessed by the building society. And the tragedy of it is that after the loss of their luxuries, the buyers continue to pay for them. For years. Sometimes for the rest of their lives.

As a credit-user, then, you may not be the carefree, successful person pictured in the advertisements. Time and again, credit, far from bringing you life's luxuries, has the effect of degrading your lifestyle until you find yourself going without *essentials* in order to meet your debts.

The solutions to debt

At that point you may, like many others, develop a kind of mental paralysis. Everything seems to be going wrong. The debts grow larger every day. You don't know which way to turn. You desperately want to start over, but the situation is so far out of control that all you can do is sit and wait for the end to come, as though you're piloting

61

an aircraft and you've suddenly forgotten how to fly.

The paralysis, of course, is part of the danger. The longer you watch the ground spinning towards you the harder it'll be to reverse the nosedive and climb back to a safe altitude. Like it or not, you are the only person who can get that aircraft out of trouble. You may need help – instructions over the radio from another pilot or air control – but it's your hand, not anyone else's, that's on the joystick. Just get it into your head that however bad the situation seems, *it is not hopeless*. There is a way out of debt. Not just a way out of the sheer financial fact of debt, but a way out of that complex arrangement of feelings and attitudes that make debt so hard to bear. In fact, if you want to overcome your debt problem, *it is vital that you tackle both at the same time.*

One reason for this can be explained by a simple illustration.

Imagine you get on the scales one morning and discover – what you've suspected for some time – that you're ten kilos overweight. You decide to diet. After all, there's no chance of shedding extra inches while you're eating all those french fries and cream cakes; dieting is about calories – specifically, about cutting them down. So in a flush of reforming zeal you consign yourself to three weeks of celery and black tea and at the end of it you're not exactly down to your target weight, but pretty close to it. The pressure's off. You've almost made it. Now you can go back to normal.

This kind of reasoning bedevils dieters and debtors alike. Of course having the firmness to stick to a crash diet is commendable. But that doesn't strike at the root of the problem. What the sensible dieter asks is not 'How can I get my weight down again?' but 'What made me gain weight in the first place?' Usually, though dietary vows are often taken after Christmas, the blame can't be pinned on one single event – if you indulge yourself at the festive season the chances are you're indulging yourself at other times too. So if you want to *keep* your weight down when the crash diet's over you will have to think carefully about your definition of 'normal' eating. Go back to french fries and black forest gateau and you'll soon be busting the bathroom scales again.

In the same way, beating debt demands two kinds of action.

One is the 'crash diet', the radical measures you have to take in order to restore your finances. As this can be very involved, and since everyone's financial problems differ, we are only going to look at the principles in this book. For personal help, far better than reading any book on debt is to approach one of the advice agencies listed in Appendix 2. They will give you accurate and detailed advice in strict confidence.

The other kind of action is a careful look at what your 'normal' life consists of. And it is to this that we turn in the next chapter.

Chapter 7

Solution 1: The New You

'If only someone would give us £2,000, or lend it to us interest free, we'd be able to clear our debts.'

A lot of people with debt problems say that. The amount varies – £2,000, £10,000, £500 – but the longing is always the same; to achieve a state of solvency where life can thrive and blossom as it did in the days when they were earning more than they owed.

But notice the assumption in this. Debt is viewed as a matter of mathematics, figures on a balance sheet that never quite add up. And of course it *is* that. You owe your various creditors a certain amount of money, the interest is being charged at such-and-such a rate, the electricity bill comes to that precise amount, and all these demands have to be met from a certain, known quantity of income. Debt is always expressed in the language of accountancy.

In contrast, however, the things that lead to and control debt have nothing to do with either money or maths. For example, the £5.00 debit that shows every month on your storecard statement did not appear by magic. It arrived because you decided to buy a new radiocassette, and to pay for it on credit.

How did you reach that decision?

There could be almost any explanation. Maybe your old machine had broken down. Or your friend had just bought one. Or somebody recommended it to you. Maybe you bought it as a present for somebody else, or simply on a whim.

Notice that none of those reasons had to do with your financial state. That's not to say you didn't take money into account. But probably the money was a limiting factor – a reason why you chose that particular model of radiocassette and not the one that was ten pounds more expensive.

Imagine an old-fashioned pair of scales, with trays and lead weights. We all have inside us a mechanism a bit like that, and we use it whenever we make a purchase. Into one tray we put all the reasons why we want to buy the radiocassette (or the jewellery or the new house, or whatever); and into the other we put different, less comfortable ones: reasons that urge us not to buy, or to buy cheaper, because we can't afford the asking price.

If the only 'weights' involved are the cost of the goods and the amount of spare cash you have in your wallet, the decision is pretty straightforward: either you can afford to buy or you can't. Credit, however, makes things more complicated. Usually, the effect of credit is to tip the scales in favour of a purchase. In view of the fact that spreading the cost of your purchases actually increases the price, this may seem strange. But then, when you're in the shop, 'As little as £5 a week' sounds a lot less daunting than a flat '£39.99'. And it's that impression that counts. 'On those terms,' you think, 'I can afford a new radiocassette, and since it's such a bargain I'll throw in a couple of blank tapes as well.'

In this way you are gently encouraged to go beyond your means. Advertising in general, as we saw earlier, tries to link your image of yourself with the image of a particular product. Credit advertising suggests to you that the product – car, dress, home improvement – is not only desirable, but *affordable*.

Clearly, then, if you get into debt through over-commitment of income – too frequently allowing the pros to outweigh the cons – you're not entirely to blame for your mistake. Society seems to demand two contradictory things: one, that you be responsible in your financial affairs, and two, that you spend irresponsibly in order to conform to the idealised image pushed at you by the advertising industry.

There is, of course, only one way in which these two things can be done at the same time, and that is: to be rich.

The wealth game

It's important to understand how we think about wealth, because wealth is tied up with nearly everything our society values.

Ideas like power, freedom, security, independence, all imply the ability to spend. If you are unable to spend, then the implication is that you are neither powerful nor free, and live an insecure existence dependent on others. In fact in Britain today it's probably more acceptable to be fat than poor. At least if you're overweight it shows you had some spare cash last time you were in the confectionery shop!

For the poor, the connection between spending power and social standing is painfully clear. If you can't afford to buy new clothes you don't just feel shabby – you feel ashamed. And the telling point is that society imposes this shame on you without a word being spoken. Your friends may completely ignore the worn elbows and scuffy shoes, yet you still sense an obligation to dress fashionably, an obligation that scant resources prevent you from fulfilling. In some obscure way you feel you've let everyone down just by not having enough money.

And this is where the credit advertiser comes into his own. 'Ah,' he says, 'but you do have money, if only you knew it. In this shop today you can spend £250 and it will cost you only £5 a week.' He will adopt a similar approach

67

with a company director. The figures are bigger, the commodity more expensive, but the principle remains the same. The client feels a need to be more conspicuously wealthy, and credit offers him an easy way to do it.

This is not to say, of course, that every purchase you make on credit is made with the speicific intention of flaunting your wealth, real or imagined. But the pressure – a kind of nationwide keeping up with the Joneses – is constant and unremitting. This is partly because it's articulated in the media, and partly because it has become a sort of game in which, willy-nilly, almost everyone in the country has joined. Every so often it comes around to your move, and you're expected to throw the dice. Buy that new dining suite. Take that fortnight in Tenerife instead of Majorca. And so it goes on.

Losers and leavers

The losers in the wealth game are the ones who get into debt. You might expect the losers to leave. But usually they don't. Most of them stay, as it were, sitting at the table, watching other players succeed, wondering what went wrong and hoping against hope that something will happen to put them back in the game. It rarely does; and anyway, people who escape debt through a windfall seldom escape it for long.

In the end there is only one way to beat debt: you have to get up and leave the wealth game.

This takes courage. And it takes conviction. After all, you've been brought up in a society that sees money as the means to every form of success. Power. Freedom. Security. Independence. If you leave the game, you're rejecting the values most other people live by. That is why it is important to start thinking about an alternative set of values right at the very beginning. For example, those who take Christ's teaching seriously – see that there is far more to life than the accumulation of goods. Even if you have no religious faith you may find it helpful to picture your departure from the wealth game as being like a religious conversion. After all, you are challenging some of your own most fundamental beliefs, knocking down the mental building you occupy and laying the foundations in a different place.

For that reason, it's important not to take this chapter lightly. The heading 'The new you' means exactly what it says. You are restructuring your attitude to life so thoroughly that it will come out of the process looking vastly different.

But how is that restructuring done? And where do you begin?

Who are you?

Think for a moment about your income.

You will probably be aware of people who are 'better off' than you are, and of others who are 'worse off'. The groups are unlikely to seem the same size: if your finances are in a mess you'll see the first group as larger; if you're doing well, the second one.

Now make a comparison between yourself and the larger group. Ask what it is that makes you feel different, what it is the others have that you want, or what it is the others don't have that you'd hate to lose. We're not concerned here with minimum basics like food, warmth, shelter and schooling for the kids. Presuming you have those, what other things really matter to you?

How you answer the question will tell you something about your place in the wealth game. How much you earn, whether you're in the black or in the red, isn't important. The key issue is how far you regard money as essential to insuring your status in society. Of course having more money is convenient, just as having less of it is inconvenient.

But would joining an exclusive club make you more at ease with your peers? Would having to buy your clothes at a thrift store make you feel inferior? Do you really in no way envy those who are richer than you or pity those who are poorer?

Remember: there's no moral judgement implied here. We're not concerned at the moment with the question of whether wanting or possessing life's luxuries is right or wrong. Nor are we saying that wealth is the only source of status in Britain today. There are others: class, intelligence and education, for example.

The issue is *our particular motivation for earning and spending money*, and in that respect not many of us can deny being affected by the way other people think of us. We are all, to that extent, players in the wealth game. How seriously you as an individual are playing only you can know. But it's important to have that knowledge. That's where you begin the fight against debt.

What really matters?

At this point some good advice is to be found in a book that at first sight has little to do with sorting out debt problems. It is the Gospel of Luke.

A prosperous man, a man with every kind of status, comes to Jesus and asks, 'What must I do to inherit eternal life?' If you are not a Christian you will probably find the idea of inheriting eternal life a little strange. That is not important. Notice the man's state of mind: being wealthy he must surely have possessed every comfort and convenience the world was able to offer him, and yet, apparently, he felt the need for something more, something beyond the reach of his money.

Jesus' reply to the rich man was extremely perplexing: 'You still lack one thing. Sell everything you have and give to the poor, and you will have treasure in heaven. Then

70

come, follow me' (Luke 18:22). Strong medicine? Perhaps. But the point Jesus makes is absolutely true: life's greatest rewards are not to be found in the vaults of the bank, in status or in the accumulation of wealth. They belong to an entirely different order.

Not that being wealthy, or even relatively well-off, is intrinsically wrong, or that Christ's advice to that one wealthy man is to be applied indiscriminately to anyone with a spare fiver in his pocket. Poverty does not guarantee faith. Jesus was talking about getting priorities straight.

Of course you may have no interest in this particular angle on the question of debt. But even if you have no desire to join the church you will have recognised by now that not everything you value has to do with the wealth game. In the end, you may say, your family, or living in a peaceful place you love, matters more to you than building your status. If you're courageous enough you may say that living a good life is your top priority, or giving something to the world through your work, voluntary service, friendship, practical skill or artistry. Even hobbies and self-improvement are legitimate alternatives to the wealth game.

In other words, with a little thought, it's not hard to find some nobler reason for living than spending money. You don't have to be somebody else's pawn; you don't have to follow blindly (just because everyone else seems to) the idea that acquiring possessions is pretty well all that matters. It's your life – why not find your own way of living? Why not put first the things *you* want to put first? Why not – and here is the crucial point – stand apart from the wealth game not because you're losing, but because the rules are bent, because the 'system' that encourages people to misuse money is actually wrong?

Be a critic

The fact is, the wealth game is played with loaded dice. If you've got into debt that may have occurred to you already. At its most basic the unfairness has to do with the way credit is advertised and administered. Because the advertiser's job is to persuade you, everything he says about credit, cars, lawnmowers, detergent or anything else, should be treated with the utmost caution. All that matters in any kind of advertising is the factual information it communicates about the product. You don't need to know, for instance, that a certain manufacturer has 'the most respected name in electronics' (respected by whom – his own sales team?), or that a new 1.2 litre hatchback does some incredible number of miles to the gallon when under normal road conditions it performs much the same as any other 1.2 litre hatchback. In credit advertising it is especially important to cut through the nonsense about privilege and membership and free offers, and to get to the hard core of terms and statistics. How much credit is being offered? What is the APR? Does the APR vary with the manner of payment? How much is the credit going to cost you if you pay it back over a realistic period? Is any security required? What are the consequences if you default? Most important – *can you get a better deal somewhere else?*

A second form of unfairness is related to the wider conditions governing credit and debt. Most people would agree that the rules under which credit and debt are regulated should have the same characteristics as those found in the Old Testament law: they should be just, and merciful, and provide the debtor with hope. Even in Britain, however, despite legislation like the Consumer Credit Act, the overall control of household debt leaves a lot to be desired.

Here are some of the major shortcomings:

1: Mis-information

Justice demands that lender and borrower treat each other fairly. But in a typical situation of debt this does not happen. On the one hand, defaulting deprives the creditor of what rightfully belongs to him. On the other hand, it can be argued that a borrower defaults, in part, because in his enthusiasm to close a sale the lender has failed to make clear the terms of the agreement. Certainly advertising at present does little to sharpen the borrower's awareness of his obligations.

2: Too easy credit

Instant credit has a lot to answer for. There is little pressure on the lender to investigate the borrower's circumstances before he makes the loan. From one point of view, of course, that is only decent respect for someone else's privacy. But in practice it results in two kinds of injustice: one, the extension of credit to people who endure enormous hardship trying to repay; and two, a substantial increase in costs to all borrowers made necessary by insurance premiums to cover the relatively high rate of default.

3: Credit price inflation

Credit card companies generally charge retailers between 1.5 and 4 percent of the value of any items bought with their card. To compensate for this loss, the retailers nearly always increase their prices. But since the credit card companies do not permit the retailers to pass on the charges only to card users, these price rises affect everybody. Consequently cash buyers are paying more for their goods than they would if eveyone used cash, and card buyers are paying less than they would if eveyone used cards. The net effect of this is to transfer probably hundreds of millions of pounds a year from cash buyers (who are generally less well off) to card buyers (who are generally more well off).

4: High interest

The difference between the base rate of interest (the rate at which banks lend to each other) and rates charged to consumers varies from around 6 percent by banks and building societies, to as much as 30 percent by high street retailers. Increased profits do not generally go towards reducing rates of interest. Yet in the rest of Europe and in the USA interest margins are far lower than they are in Britain. Why are we paying so much for our credit?

5: The balance of power

When you're in serious debt, it's you versus the organisation. Since you have almost nothing, and the organisation has assets that could run into billions of pounds, it's hardly a fair match! Worse than that, there may not be anyone on the other side who has the time or concern to treat you as an individual human being. Managers are answerable to other managers, in a chain that ends with a board of directors whose job it is to maximise company profits. The shareholders to whom the managers are answerable are often not individual people at all, but other giant corporations. Ultimately, then, you have ranged against you a system that often regards you as a blip on the balance sheet, and commands vast resources where you, the consumer, are forced to rely heavily on the help and advice of public bodies like the Citizens Advice Bureaux.

6: Debt for life

One of the most devastating things about debt is its persistence. In the Jubilee Centre's study of 1,043 cases of households in debt, the average repayment period for the unemployed was thirty years. Some banks and suppliers of credit do write off debts, either because of costs, or out of consideration for the people involved. But this is exceptional. For innumerable users of credit, instant gratification turns into debt for life. Considering that this state

of affairs is, for many, little better than being in prison, 'life'
is a harsh sentence for financial mismanagment. The National
Consumer Council has suggested that debts should be waived after
regular payment over a period of three to five years. That would
be far more humane. But the proposal does not yet enjoy popular
support.

This chapter has examined the importance of developing
a new attitude to life, a 'new you'. But that, of course,
has to be coupled with a new attitude to money management. As you'd expect, the second arises out of the first.
The next chapter explains how.

Chapter 8

Solution 2: Cash Control

Money management

Most people have at some time had to manage money. If they are married they will manage money not just for themselves, but for their husband or wife and their children. Managing money is a vital skill because, whatever attitude we take to the use of money, it is the means by which we live. It is important to manage money well.

In view of that, it's surprising how badly a lot of us do it. We're sloppy. We like to feel we're in control of our finances, but so far as real management goes we tend to rely on the professionals – our bank, our employer, our building society. Actually sitting down to keep tabs on income and expenditure seems like a chore.

We would, in fact, do well to keep in mind the first rule of cash control, which is:

Money won't look after itself.

Money, like a dog, needs regular care and attention. There's nothing particularly hard about that – you just need to get organised. Really, organisation is the key, because it is only when you have this full overview of your finances that you can make sensible decisions. That applies

77

across the board, whatever your income, whether or not you're in debt. Get organised.

Organisation begins with the obvious distinction between what you earn and what you spend.

Earnings usually come in weekly or monthly, and vary little over time. If your net wage is £600 a month, you get £600 a month regularly until the boss either gives you a pay rise or sacks you. In that way – up to a point, at least – income is predictable.

Not so with expenditures. Of course, some expenditures, like mortgage repayments, are as predictable as income. But most are less so. Fuel bills come bi-monthly or quarterly and change with the weather; housekeeping skyrockets around Christmas. And besides these the year is littered with occasional expenses covering anything from holidays to dental charges.

The irregularity of expenditure goes a long way to explaining why some people give up on organisation and instead stagger from month to month, hoping that somehow January's anticipated surplus will cancel out December's deficit. There is no necessity for this. Organisation would solve most of the problems – and cure a good many headaches without resorting to aspirin.

How is it done?

Ins and outs

First, you need to list your income and expenditures in a way that will let you compare them. You want to find out how much you earn and how much you spend *per month*.

On this basis your income will be simple to work out. If either you or your partner are employed you will almost certainly receive a payslip telling you your net monthly income. Use this as the basis for your calculation. If you are claiming Family Credit or unemployment benefit, remember that you will need to work out what your weekly instalments are worth per month. To do this, multiply the weekly figure by 52 (the number of weeks in the year), and divide by 12 (the number of months in the year). The figure you finally reach after adding up all the money you have coming in per month will be your *AVERAGE MONTHLY INCOME*. Use *CHART 1* to help you.

CHART 1: AVERAGE MONTHLY INCOME

ITEM	Amount earned	Per month, wk or yr?	Date of payment	Monthly value	Notes
Employment	£ .			£ .	
Partner's employ.	£ .			£ .	
Self-employ.(net)	£ .			£ .	
Partner's s-e(net)	£ .			£ .	
Family Credit	£ .			£ .	
Unemployment ben.	£ .			£ .	
Other benefits 1	£ .			£ .	
2	£ .			£ .	
3	£ .			£ .	
Building society	£ .			£ .	
Shares	£ .			£ .	
Lodger	£ .			£ .	
Other	£ .			£ .	
	£ .			£ .	
	£ .			£ .	
TOTAL				£ .	

Cash control would be very simple if you could spend as regularly as you earn, but of course no one does, and that makes calculating monthly expenditure a bit more difficult. Begin by listing everything you spend your money on, and putting beside each entry the monthly amount you spend on that particular item. For irregular expenditures, such as birthdays, you should decide a total for the year, and then divide by 12 to find the average. Be as accurate as you can. Refer to your past electricity and gas bills so that you won't under or overestimate the payment. Don't worry whether you've bought things in cash or on credit – what you want to find out is how much you're spending. Again, if it will help you, fill in a chart from this book. *CHART 2* gives a detailed breakdown of expenses.

CHART 2: AVERAGE MONTHLY INCOME

ITEM	Amount paid	How often	Date of payment	Who is paid	Amount /mth	Notes
Rent/Mortgage	£				£	
Rates	£				£	
Water rates	£				£	
Ground rent	£				£	
Service charge	£				£	
Community charge	£				£	
Insurance schemes	£				£	
Pension fund	£				£	
Electricity	£				£	
Gas	£				£	
Oil	£				£	
Coal	£				£	
Telephone	£				£	
Maintenance payments	£				£	

(continued)

ITEM	Amount paid	How often	Date of payment	Who is paid	Amount /mth	Notes
House repairs	£_ .				£_ .	
Redecoration	£_ .				£_ .	
Car loan	£_ .				£_ .	
Car fuel	£_ .				£_ .	
MOT	£_ .				£_ .	
Road tax	£_ .				£_ .	
Vehicle insurance	£_ .				£_ .	
Car repairs	£_ .				£_ .	
Public transport	£_ .				£_ .	
Groceries	£_ .				£_ .	
Other housekeeping	£_ .				£_ .	
Kid's pocket money	£_ .				£_ .	
Childminding	£_ .				£_ .	
Pet food	£_ .				£_ .	
Vet bills	£_ .				£_ .	
Clothing	£_ .				£_ .	
Laundry	£_ .				£_ .	
Regular prescriptions	£_ .				£_ .	
Dentist	£_ .				£_ .	
Optician	£_ .				£_ .	
TV licence	£_ .				£_ .	
TV rental	£_ .				£_ .	
Video rental	£_ .				£_ .	
Christmas	£_ .				£_ .	
Birthday presents	£_ .				£_ .	

(continued)

81

ITEM	Amount paid	How often	Date of payment	Who is paid	Amount /mth	Notes
Holiday	£ .				£ .	
Trips and outings	£ .				£ .	
Sporting activities	£ .				£ .	
Hobbies	£ .				£ .	
Records and tapes	£ .				£ .	
Toys and books	£ .				£ .	
Drinks	£ .				£ .	
Cigarettes/tobacco	£ .				£ .	
Newspapers	£ .				£ .	
Other	£ .				£ .	
	£ .				£ .	
	£ .				£ .	
TOTAL					£ .	

Note that credit repayments, including mortgage and bank loans, should not be included in your *AVERAGE MONTHLY EXPENDITURE*.

Enter them in a second list, given in *CHART 3*, covering any credit for which you are now making – or are supposed to make – regular repayments. On credit card accounts, of course, the amount you pay may be up to you. If this is the case, enter the minimum monthly repayment – the smallest amount you can pay back without incurring further penalties. What you will end up with is a summary of your credit commitments – the sums you have agreed to pay to your creditors every month.

CHART 3: MONTHLY CREDIT REPAYMENTS

ITEM		Min. repayment	How often	Date due	Who is paid	Amount /mth	Notes
Mortgage		£ .				£ .	
Second mortgage		£ .				£ .	
Secured loans	1	£ .				£ .	
	2	£ .				£ .	
Unsecured loans	1	£ .				£ .	
	2	£ .				£ .	
	3	£ .				£ .	
Credit cards	1	£ .				£ .	
	2	£ .				£ .	
	3	£ .				£ .	
	4	£ .				£ .	
Storecards	1	£ .				£ .	
	2	£ .				£ .	
	3	£ .				£ .	
	4	£ .				£ .	
Catalogues	1	£ .				£ .	
	2	£ .				£ .	
	3	£ .				£ .	
Local moneylender		£ .				£ .	
Hire purchase	1	£ .				£ .	
	2	£ .				£ .	
Others		£ .				£ .	
		£ .				£ .	
		£ .				£ .	
		£ .				£ .	
TOTAL						£ .	

If you're in financial trouble, you may have defaulted on some or all of these commitments. You'll probably be struggling with other payments too – payments you make as part of your *AVERAGE MONTHLY EXPENDITURE*. If so, use *CHART 4* to record how much you owe in arrears – on anything you pay for in regular instalments, or have obtained on credit. These are your *DEFAULT DEBTS*.

CHART 4: DEFAULT DEBTS

ITEM	Amount owed	Interest rate (APR)	Notes
Mortgage arrears	£	%	
Second mortgage arrears	£	%	
Secured loan arrears	£	%	
Rent arrears	£	%	
Rates arrears	£	%	
Electricity arrears	£	%	
Gas arrears	£	%	
Outstanding Community Charge	£	%	
Water rates arrears	£	%	
Income tax arrears	£	%	
Credit card arrears	£	%	
Storecard arrears	£	%	
Hire purchase arrears	£	%	
VAT arrears	£	%	
Unpaid fines	£	%	
Maintenance arrears	£	%	
Bank overdraft	£	%	
Other	£	%	
	£	%	
	£	%	
TOTAL	£		

Put this third list aside. It will be useful later on; but before you go any further you'll have to find out whether you're solvent on a day-to-day, month-to-month basis.

All you require now is a bit of simple arithmetic. If your financial outlook is healthy, your *AVERAGE MONTHLY INCOME* should comfortably cover both your *AVERAGE MONTHLY EXPENDITURE* and your *MONTHLY DEBT REPAYMENTS*. So add the last two up and subtract them from the first.

What do you get?

Action One on a debt budget

Anyone who's running into debt problems will find the resulting number is negative. In other words, there isn't enough money in the budget to keep up with the credit commitments. Sooner or later, that means at least one of the creditors is going to go short. Probably the warning letters have already begun to arrive.

What is the solution?

Start by taking two blank sheets of paper, and labelling one *ESSENTIAL EXPENDITURE*, the other *OPTIONAL EXPENDITURE*.

Then re-allocate each entry on your *AVERAGE MONTHLY EXPENDITURE* to one or other of the new lists. When you've done that, work through all of the entries, revising your spending estimates. This time write down not what you spend now, but the smallest amount you could spend if you were determined to economise.

The purpose of this move is to restore a distinction the advertisers have done their level best to do away with: that between needs and desires.

The failure of the modern consumer to tell these apart is one of the highest achievements of the advertising industry. They are very different: to be denied a desire may be frustrating, but to be denied a need is a matter of moral outrage. By instilling in the ordinary consumer, therefore, the idea that he or she *needs* to celebrate Christmas in a forest of glitzy decorations with a case of liquor and a twenty-two pound turkey, the advertiser achieves an impulse to buy which is out of all proportion to the actual ability of these items to capture the Christmas spirit. What are we supposed to think? That nobody got to enjoy the festive season before the invention of tinsel?

The whole idea that extravagance is something we need has been introduced to us in order to boost retail turnover and profits. It claims to make us happy; in fact it does little more than create a state of psychological dependence. We need our fix of luxury before we can be sure we've had a good time.

Consequently, dividing your needs from your desires is very far from being an exercise in self-denial. It actually enables you to release yourself from manipulation. You don't have to say yes to the advertisements. You can regulate your own spending, decide for yourself what you *really* need to purchase, and how much it's worth paying. Remember:

It's your life – *you're* in control.

You will probaly find it easier to be strict with yourself than with your wife, husband, or children. Children will miss going on a summer holiday far more than you will, and this is a good reason to weigh up the advantages of getting away somewhere for a week if you possibly can. Only you can decide where to drawn that fine line between your needs and desires. Only you know exactly what life is like for yourself and your family, and what is so essential that to go without it would cause you intolerable hardship.

To put something in the *OPTIONALS* list, of course, does

not necessarily mean that you intend to go without it. At the moment you are simply examining your priorities, and developing a new approach to using your money. Whatever your financial state, the essence of that new approach is refusing to be conned out of your cash. That's not being tight-fisted. It's knowing what you need, knowing what you want, and knowing the difference between the two.

Here are three tips you may find handy in drawing up the lists, and developing the skill of cash control:

1: If you buy, buy what's useful

Replacing an old dining table with a new one won't do a lot more than give your youngest child a brand new surface to drag his fork over. Go for what's really useful. A secondhand washing machine, for instance, will save you valuable time you'd have used up sitting in the laundrette, and will actually pay for itself in under a year. Always check your motives when you're tempted to pick up some new piece of equipment from a shop or a mail-order catalogue. Is it actually going to justify the money you're spending on it? Is it really as vital as the manufacturer seems to think? Is it going to save you time, or anxiety, or money?

2: Use resources strategically

Some purchases you make, or facilities you pay for, have knock-on effects that may increase or reduce your overall expenses. Chief among these is your house. What kind of house you choose to live in, and where it is, are enormously influential in deciding the overall pattern of your costs. How far is it from the children's school, and from your work? How heavy a mortgage are you having to raise, and how much are you likely to pay in decorating and repairs? How close will you be to the cheapest shops?

Similarly with the car. Cars cost money; and yet, especially *if you live in a remote area, possession of a vehicle can boost your chances of finding work when you're unemployed, and actually be a cheap and convenient alternative to public transport.*

3: Make money work for you

The offer of instant gratification is a ploy used by the advertisers to make you buy on credit. You don't have to wait, they say, you can have it right now.

But having it right now carries one big disadvantage: it costs you. In fact your bank account may be sagging under the burden of your purchase long after the purchase itself has been forgotten. £300 of instant credit has the habit of turning into a dreary and apparently interminable schedule of repayments – a schedule made even longer by the fact that you're being charged interest and so have more to pay.

Strangely, though, some of the same financial institutions that drain your resources through credit will just as happily build them up as investment. And since rates of interest at the moment generally keep ahead of inflation, saving your money before you use it isn't just psychologically satisfying – it's good sense. All it costs you is a little patience.

Cheap at the price?

Action Two on a debt budget

It may be that you can improve your financial situation not only by revising your expenditure, but also by increasing your income.

Since the regulations about earnings, tax, and benefits are quite complex, this section will do no more than summarise the points worth checking to make sure you're getting all the money that's due to you. To get further details inquire locally as indicated below:

1: Are you paying too much tax?

All taxpayers are eligible for some kind of allowance. In effect this is a portion of their gross income on which they do not have to pay tax. The three basic allowances, which differ in value, are: the *SINGLE PERSON'S ALLOWANCE*; the *MARRIED MAN'S ALLOWANCE*; and the *MARRIED WOMAN'S EARNED INCOME ALLOWANCE*.

Additional smaller allowances are made if: you care for a dependent relative; you have special expenses arising from your job; you are a single parent caring for dependent children; or either you or your partner have to care for a handicapped person.

Allowances are made on the basis of your tax code, which is determined by information you supply on your Tax Return. If you think you are being denied an allowance you ought to get, contact your Tax Office (if you're self-employed) or your employer's Tax Office (if you're an employee), and check it out. Both will be listed in the telephone directory under Inland Revenue.

If you've bought a home, note also that under a scheme called MIRAS (Mortgage Interest Relief at Source), you can claim tax relief on your interest payments, on up to £30,000 of mortgage. You may also be entitled to tax relief on second mortgages or home improvement loans. Again, inquire at your local Tax Office.

2: Are you earning too little?

Although many jobs in Britain are poorly paid, increasing your wages can be difficult without the support of a trades union. In the short term most people consider two other options.

One is to take part-time work. Restaurants, shops, pubs and garages often need part-time help in the evenings or at weekends. Alternatively you might find occasional work as a gardener, cleaner or baby-sitter. All these openings are available also to the *unemployed, of course, but with the disadvantage that beyond a certain level earnings can affect entitlement to state benefits. If you're in doubt about taking on a particular part-time job, check the details first with your local DHSS office, or a Citizens Advice Bureau.*

The other option is for your partner to take a job. Typically, finances are put under strain when a wife is obliged to become a professional mother. But especially with pre-schoolers, resuming work does have its cost, both in the amount of personal attention you will be able to give the children, and in the money you will need to ensure they are cared for while you're away. It is wise to give the matter some careful thought. You may be able to avert the choice by doing a job from home. But make sure before you take up this kind of work that circumstances will actually allow you to do it (for instance that you have as much spare time as you think you have), and that once you have laid out money for equipment – say, a typewriter – the job will be financially worthwhile.

3: Can you get state benefits?

In fact you don't have to be on a very low wage to qualify for state assistance.

The new Social Security law, which came into force in 1988, provides two main kinds of assistance – FAMILY CREDIT and INCOME SUPPORT. The first is aimed at wage-earning parents whose income is stretched by having a family. The second is aimed at part-time or unemployed people who need financial help. Details of these, and other more specific benefits and premiums, can be found in DHSS Leaflets FB2 Which Benefit?, *FB27,* Bringing up children?. *These and other leaflets are listed in Appendix 1 at the back of this book.*

If you're on Income Support, you will automatically qualify for maximum HOUSING BENEFIT to help cover the cost of rent or rates. You can get Housing Benefit if you're not on Income Support, but you will have to apply for it to your local council. Go to the nearest large library or Citizens Advice Bureau and ask who to contact.

4: Can you do anything else?

It might seem a strange suggestion, but if you have a spare room in a house that's expensive to maintain, a lodger may help offset some of your costs. In a university or college town, many students require lodgings during term time. Further details can be obtained from the Student Accommodation Office of the university.

Take care, however, to check with your landlord or building society that you're not infringing the lease or mortgage agreement; and be careful to make a realistic charge. Income from lodgers is taxable, and this should be taken into account even though you are able to claim against tax certain costs incurred by providing board and lodging. Consult the Inland Revenue on the tax details, and a solicitor or law centre (one that works under the legal aid scheme) on the legal commitments.

Cash help may also be available from other sources. Your employer may have a STAFF WELFARE FUND set up to assist employees who get into financial difficulties. Ask the Staff Welfare Manager or Personnel Manager. Alternatively you could approach a CHARITY. Although there is some stigma attached to 'receiving charity', the fact is that many charities have large sums of money unclaimed, and will treat your inquiry with sympathy and discretion. Go to your local Citizens Advice Bureau for further information.

Are you solvent now?

If you can find any way of boosting your income, add the increase to the figure you've already calculated for your *AVERAGE MONTHLY INCOME*.

With expenditure and income reviewed, you can see

whether the changes make any difference to your overall solvency. Do the same calculation you did before, but this time subtract from your new *AVERAGE MONTHLY INCOME* the sum of your *MONTHLY DEBT REPAYMENTS* and your *ESSENTIAL EXPENDITURE*. In effect, you are seeing how much financial stability you can achieve if you pull your belt in to its tightest notch.

Here's an example of what your calculation might look like if your debt problem isn't too severe:

Monthly debt repayments:	£325.50
Essential expenditure:	£310.00
Total outgoings:	£635.50
Average monthly income:	£700.00
Average monthly income minus total outgoings:	£ 64.50

That final figure – in this case £64.50 – is your average monthly surplus, that is, the money you have coming in which is not required to cover your essential expenditure or to keep up with regular repayments of credit.

If you've been on the knife edge but haven't run up any arrears, this surplus can be looked on as profit. You can, if you want, put it aside and invest it, or use it to finance some of the items on your *OPTIONAL EXPENDITURE* list. At first, though, you'd be wise to divide it between two other uses.

Remember that you're still paying for past credit, and that your *MONTHLY DEBT REPAYMENTS* on credit cards and storecards are at the minimum level. That probably means you're paying the interest without significantly reducing the principal. Increasing the rate of repayment on these accounts will therefore save you quite a lot of money in the long run. Remember also that the surplus is an average figure. Your actual expenses will still vary from month to month. That makes it sensible to build up a reserve of savings, against which you can 'borrow' to cover irregular expenses like Christmas and house repairs.

The secret of cash contol is always to keep track. Never let things get out of hand, or ignore a problem in the hope that it'll go away. That's how people behave when they're living on the knife edge – and that's how they get into trouble. Get wise to it. Stay in control.

Chapter 9

Solution 3: Hanging In There

If debt is severe

At the end of the last chapter we were assuming you hadn't fallen behind on credit repayments. If you *have* – in other words if you are, technically, in debt – you'll need more than just cash control to straighten your finances.

Hopefully, reorganising your income and expenditure in the way indicated in the last chapter will have produced a small surplus that can be used to catch up with the arrears. But this may not be the case. It could be that even after you've done everything you can to boost your income and reduce your expenses, you're still 'running at a loss'.

Either way, having got into trouble with debt, certain steps need to be taken. First, if you haven't done so before:

Seek expert advice.

For relevant addresses and telephone numbers go to Appendix 2 at the back of this book. Remember: it costs nothing to get help with debt – all the services we refer you to give advice and assistance *free of charge*.

But what will an adviser do to help you?

The answer is: a lot. Advisers who work in this area (for organisations like the Money Advice Centres and the Citizens Advice Bureaux) are used to handling money problems; they know how to approach creditors; and they can give you invaluable help on every kind of worry from headaches to bankruptcy. They won't think you're foolish or inadequate or a failure. They know how easily debt arises, and they are sympathetic to the smallest problem you face. In fact it is no exaggeration to say that in cases of severe debt professional help of this sort is indispensable.

What follows in this chapter is not meant as a prescription for solving serious debt. It is an outline, to help you act wisely when you get into arrears, and to give you an idea of what can be done if you simply don't have the means to pay all your creditors.

The Goliath Principle

One mistake debtors often make is to cut down the quantity of their debts by paying off the small ones first.

It's a mistake for the same reason as swatting mosquitoes is a mistake when you're sitting in a cage of tigers. There might be more mosquitoes than tigers, but it's the tigers you need to worry about – even if, for the time being, the mosquitoes are being more of a nuisance. And this is often the case. Your smaller creditors – that is, the ones who have least power to make you pay up – are the ones most likely to come knocking on your door.

When this happens it is essential to observe the Goliath Principle:

Give greatest priority to those creditors who have most power to hurt you.

The shop that issued your storecard may bother you a lot more than the building society who gave you a mortgage.

Both are making legitimate demands. But if you pay the shop *first*, you will have less money left over for the building society. And it's the building society who can really do you harm. The shop may finally take you to court; but the building society can repossess your house and leave you without a home.

So one of the first tasks for someone in serious debt is to put his creditors in order of importance. Priority debts constitute the following:

1: Mortgages/second mortgages

Any loan for which you put up your home as security – and that can be a first or second mortgage, or a secured loan – carries the risk of the creditor taking the property over if you default.

2: Rent

If you fall behind on rent payments, a landlord is entitled to obtain a court order and evict you. A lesser known, and thankfully lesser used option is distraint, under which the landlord may instruct a private bailiff to visit your home and take possession of your belongings until the rent arrears have been paid. If you don't settle within seven days the bailiff can sell your belongings through an auction house.

3: General rates

Distraint is also used to enforce the payment of rates. Failure of distraint to raise enough money for payment of rates arrears will result in your being taken to the Magistrate's court and given a prison sentence, suspended on condition that you make an agreed weekly payment towards the arrears. Further default results in imprisonment.

4: Services

The final sanction for suppliers of water, gas and electricity is disconnection. Water authorities are reluctant to disconnect because of the risks to health, but gas and electricity may be disconnected in as little as three weeks, with a deposit and reconnection charge required for restoration of supply, as well as a full payment of arrears.

5: Others

There are other, more specialised debts that incur heavy sanctions. For the self-employed, unpaid VAT can result in distraint, and income tax arrears in distraint or imprisonment. Imprisonment can also result from the non payment of maintenance by a divorced husband, and for unpaid fines.

Debt etiquette

Recognising priority debts, of course, does not mean ignoring the rest. In fact when it comes to handling creditors of all kinds you should remember that a little co-operation goes a long way. There's nothing more likely to antagonise a creditor than to leave him in the dark. So make sure to observe a little debt etiquette:

Always keep your creditors fully informed of your situation.

A person who's fallen behind on credit repayments through sudden and unexpected redundancy is more likely to win sympathy than someone who's simply stopped paying. Not that sympathy as such is what you're after. What you want to impress on your creditors is your awareness of the difficulty, your awareness of the inconvenience it is causing them, and your concern to do everything within your power to meet your commitments.

Always be courteous. Always be patient and reasonable. Always act responsibly, even when you seem to get nothing back but threats and final demands. In the end, it pays off. Nearly every creditor you'll meet will accept even a small settlement provided he knows he's being treated fairly. All you have to do is prove you're being fair.

Here the charts in the previous chapter come in very useful. Taken together your *AVERAGE MONTHLY INCOME*, your *MONTHLY CREDIT REPAYMENTS* and your *MONTHLY ESSENTIAL EXPENDITURE* form a *FINANCIAL STATEMENT* from which it will be clear you can afford to spend only a certain limited amount on debt repayments.

Take care to review the charts. A creditor you owe £500 to may ask why you allow yourself £10 per month on drinks, so you've got to be able to justify every essential expense. The *FINANCIAL STATEMENT* is your most powerful weapon here. It shows you're organised. It shows you mean business. And it proves your resources are finite.

But how much should each creditor get?

Once you've worked out how much you can spare each month to service your debts, a good rule of thumb is to divide it proportionally according to the amounts you owe in arrears to each creditor. That way the creditors to whom you owe most in arrears are receiving the largest share of repayment.

Of course the situation may have gone beyond the question of *arrears*. If you've suffered a drastic fall in income you may be unable to meet even your *MONTHLY CREDIT REPAYMENTS*. In this case you will have to calculate your *FINANCIAL STATEMENT* on the basis of *AVERAGE MONTHLY INCOME* and *MONTHLY*

ESSENTIAL EXPENDITURE, and regard your *MONTHLY CREDIT REPAYMENTS* as figures to be renegotiated alongside the arrears, covering both from whatever surplus is left once your essential expenses have been paid.

And if there's still no surplus?

In that case it is important to let your creditors know, and tell them you're willing to forgo for a while even some items on your list of essentials if they would reduce their demands accordingly. Creditors will often respond well when they know you are making a real sacrifice to repay them. Smaller creditors – ones to whom you owe less – may be willing to accept a proposal of suspended interest and nil repayments until you are able to resume normal payment of the debt. A few, in the end, may write the debt off.

The courts and bankruptcy

Ideally, you should, even if you have no surplus at all, be able to reach a negotiated settlement with all your creditors. Few creditors will waste time and money trying to force larger payments when it's clear you have numerous commitments and limited resources. On the other hand it may just be that negotiations break down, and a creditor actually takes you to court.

The workings of the judicial system, and the consequences of judicial decisions on the debtor, vary according to the area you live in – Scotland, Northern Ireland, or England and Wales. However, there are some general points to remember that apply across the whole United Kingdom:

1: The courts are impartial

Although court proceedings are generally initiated by the creditor, the courts themselves are impartial. The role of the court

100

is to provide independent arbitration between two opposing parties. It decides whether money is owed, how much is owed, and how it should be paid; if a secured loan is involved, the court will decide whether the creditor may enforce the debt by possessing your house. Consequently, going to court has one big advantage for the debtor: his case will be given a fair hearing. In fact the frequency with which the courts decide on terms favourable to the debtor is a major disincentive to creditors on the verge of legal action.

2: Keep the court briefed

When a debtor fails to attend a hearing, the court often has little alternative but to do what the creditor wants. That means it is important to co-operate quickly, fully and courteously at all stages of a legal proceeding, and to make sure that the court knows not only the circumstances of this individual debt, but your complete financial situation. Always take your FINANCIAL STATEMENT to court hearings. If you provide the court with an accurate summary of your finances it is more likely that the outcome will be fair to you as well as to your creditor.

3: Use Legal Aid

Hiring lawyers costs money, as everyone knows. Although full legal aid is available for only some court actions, you are entitled in any court action to free (or at least inexpensive) advice from a solicitor. To find out more about legal aid, or to get first hand advice on the courts, contact a Money Advice Centre, a Citizens Advice Bureau or a law centre.

The final and most desperate solution to debt is bankruptcy.

At first sight bankruptcy may seem an almost miraculous new start, since the bankrupt is generally discharged from all his debts after a period of two or three years. In practice, however, bankruptcy is traumatic. In spite of recent changes in the law protecting personal possessions, the bankrupt loses nearly everything he owns. His house, even property he inherits during bankruptcy, is realised as an asset. He lives in a state of financial suspended animation, his monetary affairs overseen by a trustee, his ability to use credit severely curtailed, hardly able to operate a bank account.

It's hardly surprising that the incidence of divorce and serious mental and physical illness is high among bankrupts. So think very carefully before declaring bankruptcy if there is still another option open to you. Ironically, if bankruptcy is your only way out of debt, it will cost you more than £100 to present the required petition to the Official Receiver's Office. It can be the meanest indignity of debt that you can't even afford to go bankrupt.

Chapter 10

It Can Be Done

Help with the emotional crisis of debt

The experience of debt can be devastating.

We indicated in an earlier chapter what life can be like 'on the inside', when debt starts to lean on family relationships, on social life, and on your sense of self esteem. To provide specific solutions to this aspect of debt goes beyond the scope of this book. Nonetheless it is important that the solutions be found, and where you look for support in this area depends a lot on your own personal background.

For the Christian there is much to be gained from prayer. Many people have found their experience of debt profoundly transformed in a way reminiscent of Psalm 23: 'I will fear no evil, for you are with me·. . .' But even if you don't feel that your religious faith is a suitable arena for dealing with the emotional traumas of debt, you may find it helpful to talk things over with a friend, a counsellor, a church minister or your family doctor. Often someone outside your situation – especially if he or she has experience of the problems you face – will be able to offer you new insights and sensible advice.

A word from the travellers

Never lose hope. As the law stands, the road out of debt may be long. But the road has an end, and many people who have got into financial trouble are now making the slow journey back to solvency. Just starting to sort things out can be a tremendous source of encouragement. John Scott, whose wife tried to commit suicide because of her debt problems, put it like this:

'As soon as I found out, I knew I needed help. I just didn't know where to start. I went to the Citizens Advice Bureau and saw one of their advisers. She was marvellous. She got it all worked out. Now I've got my wife settled down again. I'm on a very low wage, but we both know what the situation is, and we shall manage.'

Marjorie Gill's debt problems began when her husband left her. Because he gave her no support, she was forced to go out and find a job. It didn't pay well. By borrowing money she just about managed to feed and clothe her children until the doctor told her she had damaged kidneys and would have to stop work. By then she weighed a little over five stone, suffered constant pain, and had run up a string of debts. That, she says, was when everything went wrong:

'I couldn't manage. I just couldn't. That was when I went to the Money Advice Centre. I got a tremendous amount of help from the money adviser. She wrote and told people that I owed money, and told them the circumstances, and coming from her they took a lot more notice and some of them simply wrote the debts off because it was more expensive to keep sending the collectors round. My life has changed, it really has. I've taken in a lodger. With £132 in my bank account, and a Post Office account, I've cleared up my debts.'

What advice does Marjorie have for other people in debt?

'The Money Advice Centre do a marvellous job. People should go there sooner. They shouldn't hold back, or try to hide their debts because they're ashamed. I felt very embarrassed. But you don't realise how kind and understanding people can be. The longer you wait, the worse the debt becomes . . .'

To some extent, Britain's growing debt problem is the fault of the 'system'. It is encouraged by the advertisers, and by the failure of institutions like the Government to limit the availability of credit and to regulate the advertisers' behaviour. But the system can't take all the blame; in part at least, most debtors have got into trouble through their own mismanagement. There is little the Government or the Bank of England can do about that – the solution lies in individual people and their willingness to take a new, more critical approach to living in the age of credit.

If you are one of the hundreds of thousands, perhaps millions of people in Britain today who worry over credit and debt, remember: it *can* be sorted out. Finding a 'new you', getting to grips with cash control, if necessary hanging in there when the going's tough – these initiatives will help you. Just take one final word of advice:

Don't wait. Take action now.

Appendix 1

Current Government Leaflets On State Support

Details of all forms of financial assistance available through local and central government are covered in a series of free leaflets issued by the Department of Health and Social Security. Here is a list of the ones you may find most useful:

Babies and benefits	FB 8
Bringing up children?	FB 27
Child Benefit	CH 1
Family Credit	FC 1
Guide to the Social Fund	SB 16
Guide to Housing Benefit	RR 1
Guide to Income Support	SB 20
Help with NHS costs	AB 11
Income Support—Cash help	SB 1
One Parent Benefit	CH 11
Sickness Benefit	NI 16
Social Security benefit rates	NI 196
Which benefit?	FB 2

The more general leaflets are often stocked at post offices. All of the leaflets above, and a large number of other more specific ones, can be obtained at your local Social Security office. (The address and telephone number will be listed under Social Security, or Health and Social Security, in the telephone directory.) Alternatively, you can obtain leaflets by writing to the Leaflets Unit, PO Box 21, Stanmore, Middlesex, HA7 1AY.

Since the structure of the benefit system is fairly complex, you may be hard put to decide whether you're eligible for a particular benefit or not. If this is the case, you can call for free advice from the telephone service Freeline Social Security. You will not be put through to your local Social Security office. The number is: 0800-666555.

Note

The details contained in this appendix were correct on January 1, 1989, but may alter subsequently.

Appendix 2

Where To Find Help With Money Problems

The services available to advise you on debt are absolutely free. But unlike the Social Security system they are not organised in a coordinated national network. Small schemes, serving certain areas or cities, can be found in different parts of the country, but the pattern is changing so fast that it would be misleading to put a list of them in this book.

The only advice organisation with branches across the whole United Kingdom is the Citizens Advice Bureau. The branch nearest to you may or may not have an adviser who specialises in debt management. But the staff will be able to give you accurate general advice, and will certainly direct you to a specialised local scheme if one exists – for instance a Money Advice Centre belonging to an office of the Money Advice Association.

The address and telephone number of your local Citizens Advice Bureau will be listed in the telephone directory. You can phone, or simply go into the office and talk to one of the advisers.

If you live in England or Wales an additional service is available, run by the Money Advice Association and Birmingham Settlement. This is the HOUSING DEBT-LINE. The number is (021)-359-8501. You can call on Monday and Thursday between 10.00am and 4.00pm, and on Tuesday and Wednesday between 2.00pm and 7.00pm, and you will receive confidential advice from a specialist in personal debt problems. You will also be sent, free of charge, a self-help information pack which will tell you how to work out a personal budget, deal with priority debts, work out offers of payment to creditors, and cope with court papers and procedures.

Remember that it is never too soon to talk to someone about money problems. All the advice services will treat your enquiry in confidence, and will take seriously anything, however trivial, that is causing you confusion or distress.

Note

The details contained in this appendix were correct on January 1, 1989, but may alter subsequently.